THE HEBRIDES AT WAR

A Flying Fortress crew prepare for an operation on Benbecula.
(Thomson)

The Hebrides at War

Mike Hughes

Birlinn

This edition published in 2001 by
Birlinn Limited
West Newington House
10 Newington Road
Edinburgh
EH9 1QS

www.birlinn.co.uk
Reprinted 2003
Copyright © Mike Hughes 1998

The right of Mike Hughes to be identified as the author of this
work has been asserted by him in accordance with
the Copyright, Designs and Patents Act 1988

First published in Great Britain in 1998 by
Canongate Books Ltd, Edinburgh

ISBN 1 84158 143 7

British Library Cataloguing-in-Publication Data
A catalogue record for this book is available
from the British Library

Typeset by Carnegie Publishing, Lancaster
Printed and bound by GraphyCems, Spain

I dedicate this book to my late mother and father Anne and Tom Hughes and to my wife Barbara, without whom this would not have been possible.

Contents

Foreword

HAVING HAD the good sense to marry a girl with strong Oban and Tiree connections, I first visited the area with my soon-to-be parents-in-law in 1980. I was told of the magnificent scene that was Oban Bay in wartime, which my father-in-law saw regularly as a schoolboy visiting Oban from Taynuilt.

On Tiree I was amazed by the collection of wartime buildings still visible around the island. Being inquisitive by nature and having grown up in the 1960s surrounded by World War Two stories, I wanted to know more of the story of the Hebrides in wartime. In 1988 we moved to Oban and finding little in print I decided someone should try to capture the story while memories persisted. Why not me ?

Although my initial focus was on the military acitivity around Oban during the course of World War Two, it soon became clear to me that so much had happened in the isles to the west. I began to discover details about what was going on not only on Tiree, but also Islay, Colonsay, Mull, Benbecula and many other islands, and I began to appreciate the full involvement of the West Highlands and islands in the vital struggle which was the Battle of the Atlantic. While I believe this book touches on most aspects of the Hebrides

during the war, it is for other books to tell of the actions on the nearby Clyde or the secret training camps of organisations such as SOE in the Highlands. Although this record is not by any means comprehensive, what I hope to have achieved is a tribute to those who served and gave so much.

In the course of my research for this book I have talked with, corresponded with and met some delightful people from around the world. I have received a wealth of memories, both in the form of photographs and written and oral reminiscences. The images that are contained here are, I believe, filled with fascinating and sometimes poignant detail. I am aware that many of the photographs sent to me had been taken 'illegally', yet I am grateful as their record of the activities of the different armed services in Oban and elsewhere is invaluable to a book such as this.

Sad to say, some of those I have been in contact with over the course of the last few years are no longer with us, and as each member of this generation passes the world becomes a poorer place. I urge others of my generation to capture their story and something of their spirit before it too passes.

Mike Hughes
Lanarkshire, May 1998

Introduction

The Battle of the Atlantic was the dominating factor all through the War. Never for one moment could we forget that everything that happened elsewhere, on land, at sea, or in the air depended ultimately on its outcome, and amid all other cares we viewed its changing fortunes day by day with hope or apprehension. The tale of hard and unremitting toil, often under conditions of acute discomfort and frustration and always in the presence of unseen danger is lighted by incident and drama.

Vigilance could never be relaxed. Many gallant actions and incredible feats of endurance are recorded, but the deeds of those who perished will never be known.

Winston Churchill, *The Second World War*, Volume 5.

THE BATTLE OF THE ATLANTIC was the longest battle of World War Two, and, for the course of it, Scotland's north-west coast and the Hebrides represented part of the front line. The West Highlands and islands are renowned for troublesome seas, mountains, lochs, remote glens and sandy beaches. Throughout the war the shores of the region ebbed and flowed with the debris of a war out at sea. Each sinking of a Royal or Merchant ship almost inevitably found a telegram of grief at the door of one Hebridean croft or more, the son or father never to return.

The contribution made by the Hebrides, West Highlands and towns like Oban was not just that they provided a safe haven for convoys and Naval ship refits, for flying boat bases and Royal Marine training grounds. Nor was it only the outstanding record of the RAF on the island of Benbecula in U-boat attacks. Or the working up at Tobermory of Royal Navy crews for the war at sea. Neither was it just because the RAF Meteorological Squadron at Tiree provided so much crucial data, including the information which helped launch the second front on D-Day. It is all this and more.

Though but fifty or so years have passed there is such a gulf separating those days and now. Then, many Hebrideans spoke Gaelic and had little or no English. Great numbers had never even visited the mainland. There was a sense of loyalty and duty not found today, along with genuine patriotism. In the countries of the Empire ties were very strong to Britain. Lack of leisure opportunities meant service in the Territorials was popular. In a relatively large

One of the great revolutions of the inter-war years in the Hebrides was the arrival of aircraft. This was the first aeroplane to land at Tiree. Over the course of World War Two, the simple grass airstrips on many islands were upgraded for use by operational RAF units flying patrols for the convoys. (McKinnon)

Many aspects of Hebridean life were still very traditional when they were encountered by servicemen from around the world. This photograph, of a man thatching his croft, was taken on Tiree by anthropologist George Holleyman. (Holleyman)

town like Oban, horses and carts still prevailed in 1939. Aging steam trains and MacBraynes boats came and went in unhurried schedules.

At the time of World War Two Britain depended on the Merchant navy for all its supplies of oil, half of the food the country required, and most of its raw materials, to say nothing of the arms and men needed to fight a war. The sea routes were Britain's lifeline.

They were treacherous to seamen even in peacetime, but during the Battle of the Atlantic, a battlefield which was in effect millions of square miles of sea, it is estimated that over 2500 Allied merchant ships were sunk, over 30,000 merchant seamen lost their lives, 90 Allied warships were sunk and 6000 Royal Navy seamen perished. Among the airmen, Coastal Command lost 5000 men and 700 aircraft, while on the opposing side three out of every four U-boat

The Battle of the Atlantic: a convoy vessel sinks after being hit by torpedo as the remainder of the convoy proceeds in the background.

A mother and child looking at a display of a POW camp in Chalmers Store, Oban, in 1941. Many Highland men had been taken prisoner at Dunkirk. (McDougall of McDougall)

more heavily armed and regularly chose to remain on the surface and fight it out with attacking aircraft. Late in the war the Germans devised a 'Schnorkel' device which enabled them to stay below the surface even longer. This could well have been disastrous for the Allies had it been introduced earlier and not met with such well co-ordinated efforts from the RAF and Royal Navy. This struggle was to prove pivotal in the course of the war – as Churchill himself said, 'The only thing that really frightened me during the War was the U-boat peril.'

In the early days of World War Two the RAF had to depend on visual sightings of a surfaced U-boat. As the war progressed developments in radar and the use of depth charges radically improved results, along with factors like the introduction of very long-range aircraft and the growth of the Canadian Navy to fifty times its pre-war size. These all helped close what had been known as the 'Greenland Gap' or 'Torpedo Juction' in the mid-Atlantic where U-boats were originally out of range.

For the Royal Navy the early part of World War Two often meant slow, rusty escort vessels, often dating from World War One, being used to escort the convoys. Air cover and warships were only available for a few hundred miles each side of the Atlantic Ocean. In the first year or so RN crews had very little training in anti-U-boat tactics and there were many quarrels between senior RAF and RN personnel until 1941 when joint planning and operations came into effect. Corvettes and especially frigates were designed and deployed as purpose-built U-boat hunters. As the Atlantic supply routes became more secure from 1943 onwards invasion of occupied Europe and ultimately victory was a possibility.

World War One had touched the area, with Oban being used as a mine laying and sweeping base to counter the growing U-boat threat. Many other Highland ports were also pressed into service. A great price in lives was paid as the U-boat almost delivered the Germans victory. Then, as

crewmen died in action, amounting to some 20,000 men, and 400 U-boats were sunk.

The fall of France in June 1940 led to the opening up of the U-boat bases on the French north-west Atlantic coast. 1940 and 1941 were what the U-boat crews called the 'Happy Days' when sinking Allied ships was relatively easy. U-boats could crash dive in thirty seconds and they adopted the 'Wolf Pack' method of hunting in groups to maximise the sinkings they could inflict on a convoy. The Germans had cracked British codes and they would lie in wait for a convoy in a line covering a distance of up to 100 miles. At first the U-boats also worked in tandem with Focke Wolfe 200 Condor long-range reconnaissance bombers which could operate 1000 miles out into the Atlantic, although fortunately for the Allies this partnership was not fully exploited. As the war progressed U-boats became weapons, equipment and technology made advances through the 1930s, it became clear that any global conflict would encroach upon areas like Scotland's Atlantic coastline. Before the war the RAF tried out many locations for flying boat bases and singled out Oban, among others such as Islay, Loch Erne in Northern Ireland, the Clyde and Stranraer. Royal Navy battleships were also frequently seen in these waters in the 1920s and 1930s. It was clear that the deceptive shelter of the bays and the depopulated glens proved attractive to military planners.

The contribution of the Hebrides, however, was not just in providing safe haven. A long and honourable connection with the sea meant that many Hebridean men were absent on convoy duties with the Royal or Merchant navies, and on land the 51st Highland Division paid a heavy price at Dunkirk and St Valley. They helped buy the country time, but for so many Highlanders it meant five years as a POW.

For many of the Allied visitors to the West Highlands and Islands what remains most potent in their memories is the genuine warmth of welcome, the dignified quiet support. The potential for real problems existed, with so many visitors in the area and so many locals on active service elsewhere. That it did not transpire, that these communities existed side by side in harmony and united in desire for victory is just one of the vital factors in the defeat of Fascism and Nazi Germany.

This books presents one piece of the jigsaw of Allied success. It tells the story of locals, islanders, civilian war workers, airmen and groundcrew, sailors, WAAFs and Wrens and a few more besides. From the dark early days of the Phoney War to the launch of Allied retribution in 1942 and the build up to D-Day, Scotland's north-west coast and the Hebrides was a first and last sight of land for countless thousands during the war – the first sight for weary troops having travelled sometimes half-way round the world, and for merchant and RN sailors and Coastal

A guard from 304 (Polish) Squadron stands lonely sentry on the airfield on Tiree. (Solecki)

Command air crews perhaps the last sight as they set out to supply and protect.

From the Butt of Lewis to Kintyre it could be the last sight of land for those with no known grave but the mighty sea. Just a little piece of land, a group of islands from which at one point in World War Two shone out to the world a lonely light for democracy.

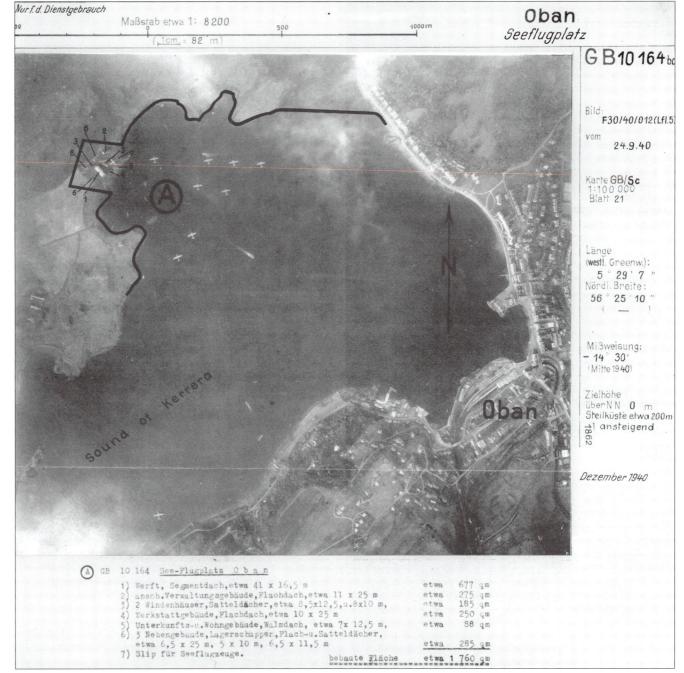

An aerial view of Oban Bay taken by the Luftwaffe in December 1940, just before an air raid. The detail the Luftwaffe intelligence listed at Kerrera was in fact remarkably accurate. (Royal Commission on the Ancient and Historical Monuments of Scotland)

1

RAF Operational Base, Oban, 1939–1943

F LYING BOATS first began using Oban Bay as a base during the 1920s and RAF activity began to increase through the 1930s as the likelihood of another large scale world conflict grew. In 1917 the U-boats had almost turned World War One Germany's way. It was recognised that the North Atlantic supply routes would be of great importance for Britain's survival and success in any future war. With a lack of long-range land-based aircraft or airfields on the western seaboard of the UK in 1939–41, flying boats had a vital role to play in shepherding convoys, making anti-U-boat patrols, searching for survivors and guarding against German long range aircraft attacks.

In October 1939, 209 Squadron of RAF Coastal Command was the first operational squadron to be stationed in Oban. When they arrived they were equipped with biplane Supermarine Stranraer flying boats, but began to convert to Saunders Roe Lerwicks in December. The old Stranraer was not heavily armed but was regarded with affection; not so the Lerwick, or 'flying pig'. Bulky and under powered, it looked in some ways like a Sunderland with two engines, but it proved to have been rushed into production much too quickly in the build-up to war. Although the Lerwicks notched up at least two bombing attacks of suspected

A Stranraer flying boat of 209 Squadron off Kerrera. The CO of 209 was Wing Commander Wigglesworth whose exploits in World War One are believed to have partly contributed to the character of the hero in the Biggles books. (Andrew)

Some men of 209 Squadron of RAF Coastal Command at Oban Railway Pier in 1938 on a pre-war visit. (Andrew)

A Lerwick being moored in Oban Bay. In the early war years, the patrolling and protection of the Hebrides by sea and air was mainly carried out from Oban, the largest base in Northwest Scotland. (Thomas)

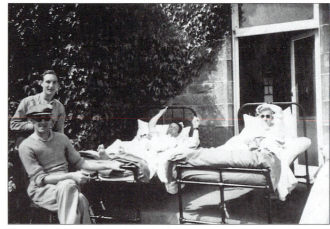

The West Highland Hospital, Oban, in wartime. The RAF and later the RN set up their own medical centres in the town. (Pearce)

An ambulance at Soroba Lane, Oban, early in the war. (Oban War and Peace Museum)

U-boats in the first half of 1940, problems were evident: on 20 February a Lerwick collided with the rocky promontory at Lismore lighthouse with the loss of five of its crew, and on 29 June a Lerwick overturned and sank taxiing to its mooring in Ardentrive Bay, Kerrera.

Jack Foord was posted to Oban on 9 September 1939 to help set up the RAF station sick quarters. 'No one at my previous base could find "RAF Oban" in the list of RAF stations or establishments so I was the subject of some leg pulling. After a very slow train journey through the dark, I reached my destination about six in the morning. I found myself and kit on a railway platform at a pier. No-one could tell me where to report. Eventually a policeman took me to the Oban Inn and told them to accommodate me – on the orders of The War Office!

'The Station CO was in the process of getting RAF Oban up and running from the Station Hotel [now the Caledonian Hotel]. Until our own Medical Officers arrived the CO arranged for a local doctor to act as Medical Officer.

RAF HQ at Dungallan House, to the south of Oban, seen from a Sunderland. As RAF Oban grew in numbers, Norman Marshall found himself posted to the Signals section at Dungallan where convoy and U-boat information came in. 'There were about a dozen wireless sets constantly tuned to aircraft and ships. We were an integral part of Western Approaches command, linked to Derby House, Liverpool.' (Thornton)

Gradually more and more personnel arrived: officers, airmen, and a contingent of WAAF personnel. The hotels on the front, Marine (now the Regent), Park, Esplanade and Great Western, were requisitioned and furnished with RAF equipment and the hotel contents stored away.

'The first medical centre was the entire first floor of the Marine Hotel, and the Marine Hotel dining room became an Airmen's mess. Many senior officers brought their families to Oban and rented furnished houses. The headquarters had taken over Dungallan House and the Group Captain and his admin staff were situated there. On Pulpit Hill nearby, there were wireless masts and radio beacons as wireless operators were located on Tiree and Skye. For the flying boats and marine craft the Isle of Kerrera slipway was

taken over. When later the RAF Regiment [who performed guard duties at RAF establishments] came into being, a detachment was stationed on Kerrera and a Nissen hut built with a gun emplacement on a hill at the harbour entrance. To take care of the general stores and equipment, the Argyleshire Gathering Hall was requisitioned early in

A photograph taken of Terry Andrew, a member of 209 in Oban, with a homing pigeon (used to safeguard against radio signals being picked up) on board a Lerwick. When asked to find a suitable site for the RAF photography dark room, Andrew chose the ladies' cloakroom in the Argyleshire Gathering Hall. Convoy vessels and possible blockade runners were photographed and processed for Intelligence at Dungallan House HQ. (Andrew)

A Saunders Roe Lerwick off Kerrera showing its rear turret. The house behind is Mount Pleasant, a distinctive landmark on the island, which was occupied by the RAF and then Italian prisoners-of-war during the war years. (Hood)

An RAF crew off duty in Oban with McCaig's Tower in the background. These lads were later lost when their Catalina went missing on Atlantic patrol. (Stewart)

October '39. The parachute section took over a church hall on Argyll Street.'

Bill Hood was also with 209 Squadron when they arrived at Oban. 'What a delight for the men. Hotel luxury in the Marine, civilisation, friendly local people, beautiful scenery and an atmosphere vibrant with history. Initial drawbacks included severe restrictions on liberty as all ranks had to be back by bedside by 9 p.m. However as social contacts locally progressed, dummies in beds and easy access by drainpipe and basement window became the order of the day. The local cinema was very popular with the RAF and at that time it boasted a tearoom. Pubs closed at 9 p.m. There were no females in pubs and beer was expensive at 6d per pint. After one good dance on my way to night duty on our "kite", I fell from the North Pier clutching a loaf of bread and my gas mask!

'At this period aircrew were made up of officers or NCO pilots and all other crew members were aircraftmen, such as Wireless operator/gunners, Rigger/gunners, Engine fitter/gunners etcetera. These lowly rankers were paid an extra shilling a day flying pay and an additional sixpence a day if qualified gunners.'

In July 1940, 210 Squadron arrived at Oban to replace 209. They stayed until February 1942, a period which coincided with the darkest days of the Battle of the Atlantic and indeed the bleakest in the whole course of the war for the Allies. Nonetheless, 210 made a valuable contribution with at least thirteen U-boat attacks in Sunderlands and, from spring 1941 onwards, Catalinas.

George Smith was a WOP/AG (Wireless Operator/Air Gunner) with 210 Squadron. 'The local people of Oban treated us in a very friendly manner, and many of us were invited to their homes. In 1940, the town still had summer visitors on holiday. Sometimes after convoy escort, we used to land outside the harbour and then taxi to our moorings. People walking along the front would wave to

A view of Oban Bay in 1941 looking west showing drifters and trawlers off the North Pier and flying boats in Ardentrive Bay off Kerrera. (Ryder)

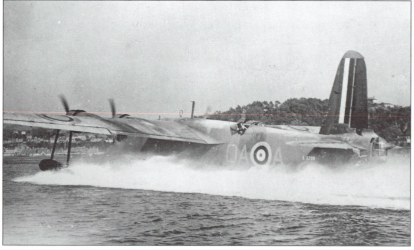

A Sunderland taxiing past Dungallan House. Built by Short Brothers, the mighty Sunderland was referred to by the Germans as 'the flying porcupine' because of the number of guns it carried. (Head)

A rare picture of a 'G' boat, one of the Empire flying boats flown by Imperial Airways before the war which was trialled at Oban and Bowmore on Islay as a potential military aircraft but not brought into operation. The photograph shows the unusual double dorsal gun turrets on the aircraft, which is moored in Kerrera Sound, below Dungallan, and an ASR boat passing by. Taking the photograph would have been highly illegal during the war, and there are instances of jail sentences and court martials for just such activities. (Saunders)

A Sunderland taking off in Oban Bay, 1940. The experience was described by air crews 'like going across a ploughed field at a hundred miles an hour'. (Barker)

An RAAF man loading depth charges onto a bomb scow. (Thornton)

us and this used to lift our spirits, more so if the trip had been rough.

'Every day two aircraft were on stand by ready to fly at short notice. When the order was received the Captain of the aircraft would then arrange for an early call for his crew usually between 2 a.m. and 3 a.m. Each member had a task to do. Two would collect rations from the mess while two more filled water drums with fresh water. Two wireless operators collected the spare 12-volt batteries. The aircrew would then go to the jetty to be taken by dinghy to the aircraft. The officers of the crew, Captain, Second Pilot and Navigator would be ferried to the aircraft separately after briefing. The Captain issued the instructions and then all members proceeded to carry out checks prior to take off. In the meantime, Marine Craft section had arranged a flare path for take-off.

'It usually took three to four hours to arrive at the location of a convoy. An Aldis lamp message would be flashed to the Naval vessel in charge to identify ourselves. The patrol would then commence keeping a sharp lookout for enemy aircraft or U-boats, flying above the ships at about 1000 feet round and round lasting about five hours. When it was time to return to base, the Captain would fly low, dipping his wings in salute and the ship crews on deck would give a cheerio wave. The crews on the merchant ships were much worse off – they were at the mercy of the sea and constant attack from submarines and enemy aircraft. At least after twelve to fourteen hours flying we were back on dry land.

'With 210 Squadron I mostly flew with Flying Officer Meggitt. He took over another crew for one trip in December 1940. On returning from patrol they crashed on landing at night after hitting an empty horse box [which had come from a convoy bombed at Oban] and only one crew member survived.'

Tom Lennox, a fitter with 210, recalls how versatile ground crew had to be. 'When a Sunderland returned to Oban minus a float, along with some other ground crew I had to take a small boat below the Sunderland wing just as it landed and hold it up with a rubber dinghy over our heads, to avoid it capsizing. This was done on a choppy sea as the Sunderland taxied at speed and propellers turned just inches from our faces.'

Denis Stone, a Wireless Operator with the RAF in Oban in 1940/41, remembers: 'I flew mostly with Van der Kiste while with 210. In some ways life on a flying boat Squadron was unique. Our roots stemmed from days when "Boats" were part of the Royal Navy in World War One. We were both sailors and airmen. We were unique in that we played a prominent part in the aircraft maintenance, unlike the air crews of land-borne aircraft who did the flying while the ground staff did all the maintenance. We looked after the

A Catalina taxiing in Oban Bay. The Catalina was manufactured in the USA (where it was known as the PBY) and in Canada. The flying endurance and range of the Catalina made it a great favourite. Perhaps the most celebrated action during this period was when 210 Squadron Catalinas were involved in shadowing the Bismarck *which helped contribute to her eventual sinking in May 1941. (Thornton)*

The blister gun turret on a Catalina. (Davis)

of control. It was quite a scene: the shepherd, the dogs, Woolworth's staff, and us, all trying to persuade the sheep to leave!'

In early 1941 American volunteers arrived in Oban to instruct on conversion to Catalinas. Ken Thomson, part of the 210 Squadron ground crew, remembers one incident: 'Some of us were visiting the cinema on a leisure evening when at about 2130 hours the film was brought to a stop and a notice was put onto the screen requesting 210 maintenance personnel to report at the North Pier immediately. There was a hurried exit and we boarded a pinnace for Kerrera. We were ferried out to two "Cats" that had just returned from an operation shadowing the *Bismarck* and been airborne for twenty-seven hours. It was a glorious evening: the bay was like a mill pond, the sun low in the sky to the west. We had to carry out maintenance inspections. The crews were taking a short spell ashore for debriefing and respite and had volunteered to rejoin the Bismarck fray as soon as possible.'

engines and airframe, the wireless equipment and the guns. We knew the techniques of mooring, anchoring, and other boat-craft. After landing there was another hour or two of re-feulling and clean-up – it could be a very long and tiring day. Additionally, two of us slept aboard in turn.

'We spent hours patrolling around convoys searching for submarines. We found one U-boat who crashed dived when he sighted us. We signalled to a Naval escort vessel which attacked and I believe sank the intruder. Once on our way back from patrol we were advised that Oban was fog bound and we were told to land elsewhere and wait for the fog to clear. The skipper chose to head for Stornoway. Some of us went ashore and found a Woolworth's store – we went in and soon were joined by a flock of sheep that had got out

Roy Davis was an aircrew Rigger on a Catalina at the time. 'On 26 May 1941 we took off in pursuit of the *Bismarck*. Flight Lieutenant Percy Hatfield was pilot. We located her at 2350 hours while flying at 4000 feet. We flew into heavy flak with black puffs of smoke all around us and the hull, a wing and aerial were all damaged. We circled all night at 1500 feet. We returned to Oban and landed after a flight of 31 hours 15 minutes (then a record I believe).

The man whose flying boat crew spotted the Bismarck, *Dennis Briggs, at Ganavan, Oban, in 1940.* (Andrew)

The wreckage of a 10 RAAF Squadron Sunderland at Kerrera. On landing in poor weather, the pilot found that the flare path had drifted too close to shore and, unable to pull up short, had crashed into rocks off Lismore. The wreckage was then towed back to Kerrera for salvage. (Hodgkinson)

Reg Williamson (far right) with crewmates on the roof of the Marine Hotel in Oban. Williamson was awarded the DFM (the ribbon is on his tunic) for shooting down a Condor from the rear turret of his Sunderland when badly wounded. (Gooding)

'On 2 September we spotted two U-boats on the surface. One dived and the other opened fire. We dropped three depth charges but our skipper was hit and the hull badly holed. Back at Oban we landed and taxied straight up on to Ardentrive beach to avoid sinking.'

William Head also flew with 210 on Catalinas. 'We sometimes went from Oban via Sullom Voe and then to Murmansk or Archangel escorting convoys. We never saw a town in Russia. They didn't speak English and none of us spoke Russian. Then came a long journey home just endlessly watching and hoping the poor devils below in the Merchant Navy would make port.'

Jim Robertson has other poignant recollections of this time: 'In February 1941 I was posted to 210 Flying Boat Squadron as a General Duties NCO. My duties were discipline and administration. From time to time we had fatal casualties due to flying boat crashes. It was one of my jobs to collect all Air Force kit and private possessions of the deceased from their rooms along with an officer. Air Force kit was returned to barrack stores and an inventory was made of private possessions. Letters had to be read in case anything which came under the Official Secrets Act was ever mentioned. This sad task I performed about five times.

'On one occasion a chap had a number of letters from his wife and ones from a girlfriend. I suggested to the officer on the task with me we destroy the letters from the lady friend but he was adamant that everything must be returned to the next of kin (his wife). I waited until the evening and went back and undid the packed box, and removed and destroyed the lady friend's letters. Regulations sometimes had to be broken.'

One tale of magnificent bravery is that of Sergeant Reg Williamson of 210 Squadron. In January 1941 Fl/Lt Aikman was flying a Sunderland on convoy patrol when a F-W Condor attacked. Its cannon scored hits on the Sunderland and Williamson in the rear turret was wounded. Despite this he held on until the Condor came within range of his

An RAF funeral at Pennyfuir Cemetry, Oban, of one of the crew members who died when a Sunderland ran into problems off Tiree in September 1942. (Chadwick)

An RAF crew on stand-by at Dungallan House (RAF HQ) garden. A Catalina is behind in the Sound of Kerrera. (Davis)

guns. He only then opened fire and the Condor was shot down. The turret was so badly shot up that the Sunderland had to be towed to Oban's North Pier. Coming to rest with the turret over the pier, Williamson had to be cut free. He was awarded the DFM and Aikman the DFC. Williamson later volunteered for a tour on Bomber Command and was lost on a flight over Germany.

In March 1942 228 Squadron arrived at Oban with their Sunderlands. They kept up the stout work of previous Squadrons with further U-boat attacks, but the cost in terms of lives of crew and in aircraft was very evident. Five aircraft were lost including one incident on 5 September 1942 when a Sunderland returning from patrol had to put down at Vaul Bay, Tiree, due to a shortage of fuel. The pilot attempted to make a run to shore but hit a rock. The crew took to the dinghy but were blown out to sea. Seven bodies were recovered and only two men survived. Two bodies were never found. One of those who died was Fred Nancarrow, a journalist with the *Glasgow Herald* who was writing a book about Coastal Command, having previously written one on Glasgow's Fighter Squadron.

Joe Ayling was a WOP/AG with 228 Squadron. 'I was put on the crew of Flying Officer Briscoe and on the second trip with him we sighted a U-boat, half submerged. I was in the tail turret, and saw the four depth charges drop very close to the U-boat's swirl. The sub had disappeared by now, but the subsequent explosions, occurring one after the other, threw mountains of water into the air. I suppose we will never know for sure whether it survived or not.'

Alan Lacy was another WOP/AG with 228 Sqn at Oban. 'The Sunderlands were always manned day and night for security by members of the crew. The total Sunderland crew was twelve. It consisted of two or three pilots, a navigator, two flight engineers, two wireless operators, two air gunners, a rigger and a wireless/electrical mechanic. Life at Oban consisted of being at various states of readiness: Strike

The wreckage of Eddie Chadwick's Sunderland which crashed at Lochboisdale in May 1942. (Jenner)

– these crews occupied the strike hut which was on high ground at Dungallan House near the operation rooms. They were ready for immediate take-off.

First Available – these crews had to stay in the mess so that they could be contacted at once if required.

Second Available – these crews had to record in a book where they could be contacted. I regret that a not uncommon entry was "Snogging in McCaig's Folly". This could result in a messenger being dispatched up the hill to call out the name of a crew member required!

Third Available – these crews could go anywhere but had to be back by midnight. In general there was not much spare time, we lived for our leave which as aircrew was one week every six weeks.'

Eddie Chadwick, a 228 Squadron wireless operator, was involved in one of the tragic crashes which occurred during this time. 'On 4 May 1942 we flew to Lochboisdale to ferry two naval officers from Oban to the Outer Hebrides. On our first approach it was realised that we didn't have

enough room as there were some nasty cliffs at the far end, so it was decided to go round again. Our second approach was very low indeed, just missing the chimneys of the houses round the harbour, and we touched down beautifully but, unfortunately, the starboard float hit what I assume to be a rock just below the surface and was either knocked off or very badly damaged and the pilots immediately decided to take off again. I can see now Squadron Leader Hollins pushing forward the four throttles whilst the skipper pulled back on the stick. We started a climbing turn (to avoid the cliffs) and I realised our climb was too steep and that we were about to stall so I took up a crash position at my wireless operator's station just behind the first pilot. I was knocked out by the impact and came to

A Sunderland under repair on the slipway at Kerrera. (Thornton)

A Sunderland coded 'M' at Oban in 1942. It may be the flying boat which later crashed with the Duke of Kent aboard in one of the most controversial incidents in Oban during the war. (Carlisle)

Frank Goyen (standing) with three of his crew alongside his Sunderland (its Kangaroo motif is shown below) which crashed with the Duke of Kent on board. (Ayling)

underwater. I could see daylight above and was able to struggle through the wreckage and reach the surface where willing hands pulled me onto the wing. We hit the edge of a small island in the loch and settled in about twelve to fifteen feet of water, thus enabling us to escape and avoid the risk of fire. The whole front of the plane up to the leading edge was very badly damaged and the back was broken, although the rear of the plane was not in the water. If we had hit the middle of the loch we would probably have gone down to a great depth with many more casualties. Eventually a boat arrived with some soldiers who got us ashore and we were taken to a convent where we were cared for by nuns and the following day we were transported to an Oban hospital. Squadron Leader Hollins and Pilot Officer Jones died and other crew members suffered extensive injuries.'

George Gilfillan was an Engineering Officer with 228 Squadron. 'I saw my first flying boats from the train as it came round the curve above the town of Oban. I was

Frank Goyen (front row, centre) with some of the Sunderland crew who died along with the Duke of Kent. The one survivor (Andrew Jack, the rear gunner) is in the back row second from the left. (Watkins)

responsible to the CO for the servicing of ten Sunderland flying boats and the supervision of about a hundred trades-men. My job was to plan inspections, estimate repair times, have modifications carried out and ensure aircraft docu-ments were maintained. I was 22 years old. Servicing was a constant battle against the effects of salt water. Work went on at moorings, irrespective of weather. We had no power tools. Drilling, riveting and metal cutting was done by hand. Insufficient tribute has been paid to those airmen. They lived in cramped billets with poor drying facilities and laboured for weary hours throughout the war, often wet, cold, and exhausted, to keep the Coastal Command flying boats in the air. Information on operations was censored so the men had not even the satisfaction of knowing the results of their labours.

'By the end of the year the Squadron moved to Lough Erne in Northern Ireland. We taxied out into the Firth of Lorne at dawn and took off in foul weather. It was raining heavily and the cloud base was at a few hundred feet. Oban disappeared in the mist.'

The most controversial event linked to Oban in wartime was the death of HRH The Duke of Kent and all but one of the people on board Sunderland 'M' of 228 Squadron. Two Australians, Flight Lieutenant Frank Goyen and the CO of 228, Wing Commander Thomas Moseley, took off from Oban with a hand picked crew and collected the Duke of Kent and his entourage at Invergordon. They were bound for Iceland but crashed near Dunbeath in Caithness on 25 August 1942. In Oban there was grief, astonishment and disbelief following the crash. Frank Goyen, the skipper, was a highly respected flying boat captain, but despite the wealth of experience in the specially chosen crew the navigator had flown only one previous operational flight. 'M' had been regarded as a jinxed aircraft by some at Oban and had recently suffered slight collision damage.

Back at Dungallan WAAF Dorothea Gray remembers civilian Met forecasters being immediately transferred to the RAF and thus subject to military jurisdiction. The CO dumped a bag in her room and told her she had to cata-logue the contents, which were personal effects from the crew. She remembers that she could not remove the smell of charring from her hands, clothes and room for weeks.

Engineering officer George Gilfillan was wakened ab-ruptly on the night of the crash and ordered to Kerrera to hand over all documentation on the flight. Many believe there was a cover up of the facts and official secrecy has led to numerous rumours abounding to this day regarding the truth of events. Goyen, Moseley and two crew mates lie in Pennyfuir cemetery, Oban.

George Street in Oban during the war after an early morning snowfall. From January to July 1943 Oban played host to 330 (Norwegian) Squadron while they re-equipped with Sunder-lands. Colonel Alf Steffen-Olsen remembers reading that 'The Norwegian Armed forces shall be used in the defence of the UK for the purpose of regaining Norway.' He also remembers that 'We were under operational control of the RAF. After two years at Iceland Oban was a marvellous change. We got an outstanding reception from the town's people.' (Thornton)

Two pre-war Judges postcards showing warships mixing with working and pleasure craft in Oban Bay.

2

Oban Royal Naval Base

ON 6 FEBRUARY 1940 the Admiralty decided that Oban should be used as an additional Naval base to Kyle of Lochalsh, which was a gathering point for convoy ships but could not provide the facilities that Oban could. On 4 April Commander AG Boyce RN (retired) was appointed Boom Defence Officer, Oban and Lochalsh. The Oban base was well positioned between Western Approaches Command to the south at Liverpool and the Clyde, and other RN bases to the west and north such as Londonderry and Loch Ewe.

One of the first RN men to establish himself at Oban was a young officer, Eric Beesley who was Captain's Secretary (Adjutant). 'I think it would be correct to describe the Naval Base at Oban as relatively small but quite important due to the variety of activities carried out there, and its location. The role of the Navy was to protect and administer the harbour and surrounding waters, to accommodate merchant ships in the anchorage and organise the sailing of the convoys to join with larger convoys to the USA, Russia and elsewhere. The Naval Officer in charge was based at the Station Hotel with his executive staff, convoy staff, communication staff, finance and secretarial staff.'

Patrols of the entrances to Oban Bay were begun by the drifters *Lydia Long* and *Apple Tree* which were requisitioned and brought into RN service. Between May and August 1940 anti-torpedo and anti-submarine boom defences were laid at the northern entrance to Oban Bay and in Kerrera Sound by HMS *Guardian*. The naval detachment at Oban grew as France fell and more and more convoys were rerouted from the English Channel and South of Ireland to the waters between Northern Ireland and Scotland.

The convoys would congregate in the area between Lismore lighthouse and Appin. The first convoy to depart from Oban was OBO 237, which left on 1 November 1940, and the first inward convoy, SL58, arrived at Oban on 26 January 1941. Shortly afterwards, Oban was commissioned as a separate base on 31 March 1941 as HMS *St Andrew*, although after some confusion with a similar name within the RN structure this was changed to HMS *Caledonia* two

A picture showing Royal Naval ships on exercise before the war in the Firth of Lorne. They are believed to be HMS Hood *(right), HMS* Repulse *(centre) and a French ship,* Dunkerque *(left).* Hood *and* Repulse *were sub-sequently lost with almost all hands,* Hood *in the Denmark Straits and* Repulse *off Singapore, while the* Dunkerque *was sunk at Oran. (McAulay)*

years later. In May 1941 Hemsley Bell Ltd were given the contract to requisition the derelict slipway at Gallanach for repairs to drifters, Motor Torpedo Boats (MTBs) and other small vessels from Coastal Forces.

In October and November 1942 the Oban area played a part in the preparations for the first major Allied invasion, Operation Torch in North Africa. Loch Na Keal on the north-west of Mull was used for berthing large transport and hospital ships while mock landings were carried out around Oban. Such activity became more common as the war progressed, and the exercising of landing craft and crews in the early months of 1944 became a common sight around north-western coasts. In addition, there was a gradual build up of so-called 'block ships' (which would be sunk as part of the mulberry harbour on D-Day) at Oban

between March and 31 May 1944. Eventually, fifty-one merchant ships, escorted by six corvettes, six trawlers and six tugs set out for the D-Day landings. Around the same time almost as many US liberty ships (the name given to the vulnerable but vital convoy ships hastily built in the

Clyde paddle steamer Aristocrat *(previously called* Talisman*) on anti-aircraft duty, Loch Na Keal.* (Polglaze)

The conning-tower of RN subs in Oban in the late 1930s. Subs such as these were deployed to check that Irish ports were not being used by German U-boats or ships. (McNeil)

USA to provide hundreds of extra merchant ships for the North Atlantic convoy routes) had gathered in the Firth of Lorne.

Although a flotilla assembled at Oban for sailing to the Far East in July 1945 the Naval station itself gradually closed down between November 1944 and June 1945. RN Oban was 'paid off' on 30 September 1945.

During their time in Oban, the Royal Navy requisitioned part of Station Hotel (as HQ), the Royal Hotel (for ratings) and the Palace Hotel, Raasay Lodge and Glencampa Hotel, all of which were used as Wrens (Women's Royal Navy) quarters. The Crown Hotel became the NAAFI, Wellpark Hotel was sick quarters, Alexandra Hotel was used by officers for accommodation, DEMS (Defensively Equipped Merchant Ships) gunners were in the Columba Hotel for a time and the Maritime Artillery was in the Argyll Square church hall. Meanwhile, signal stations were established on the South (Railway) Pier and on the Ganavan Road, with a further station on Lismore. There was also a barrage balloon section on Lismore.

Royal Navy Signals station on the Railway Pier. (Hanson)

The anti-submarine boom defence minefield laid in Kerrera Sound in August 1941. The control tower for the minefield was at Gallanach and was operated by RN officers and ratings, with the guard provided by a Royal Marine detachment who manned gun posts around what is now a caravan park at Gallanach. One row of mines mysteriously blew up on 28 September 1941 – it is rumoured that this was the work of an RN officer who was showing his girlfriend around the control tower and inadvertently pressed the release mechanism. (Barker)

(Far right) Mrs Mary McNiven of Dunstaffnage cottage with the racehorse, Bradshaws, which she rescued after the SS Breda was sunk in 1940. (McNiven)

The RN Patrol Service trawler Southern Star *at Oban.* (Hilliard)

An RN funeral procession at Corran Park, Oban. Two points of interest are the anti-invasion trenches in the foreground and the fact that some of the detail on the left-hand side has been whited out by the censor. It is likely there would have been an RN vessel or flying boat in view. (McFarlane)

During the war, Oban suffered only one effective air raid when shipping was attacked by Heinkel bombers in the Firth of Lorne on 23 December 1940, although long-range German bombers did cross the area on a number of other occasions and bombs were dropped on Shian, Loch Aweside and near Salen on Mull. In the Christmas 1940 bombing five ships suffered damage from very near misses. Of these, the SS *Breda*, a Dutch ship with a valuable cargo which had been due to go in convoy to India, was in greatest danger of sinking and was towed by a tug to Ardmucknish Bay, Benderloch, and beached. However, she gradually eased back into the water and sank. On her deck there were some thoroughbred horses which belonged to the Aga Khan. Some of these escaped in the commotion while others drowned in their horse boxes. Mrs Mary McNiven of Dunstaffnage Cottage and Miss Kate McPherson of Dunstaffnage Mains Farm rescued one racehorse (called Bradshaws) the morning after the bombing along with a dog which was clinging to a horse box. Both received SPCA awards for bravery. There are strong rumours that, believing an invasion was imminent, a Home Guard detachment fired on some of the horses still tethered to their horse boxes and struggling to reach the shore. Four days after the air raid a Sunderland coming into land struck a semi submerged horse box ripping open its hull and eleven of the twelve crew died as the flying boat sank.

To counteract the threat of further air attacks, heavily armed warships arrived to guard the Firth of Lorne, followed by 297 (Inverness) Battery of the Royal Artillery, who set up anti-aircraft gun positions at Lochnell Castle, Benderloch, and on Lismore.

RN Patrol Service

The RN Patrol Service was made up from a diverse collection of trawlers, drifters, boom defence and other vessels

Southern Star *off Kerrera setting off to assist a convoy.* (Hilliard)

The trawler Euryalis *coming to the assistance of a ditched Sunderland in May 1945 in the North Atlantic.* (McLaren)

which were commandeered by the Navy and stationed at ports like Oban during the war. They were affectionately known as 'Harry Tate's Navy' after a bumbling music hall comedian of the time. In 1940 and 1941 Harry Woods served on HMS *Norina*, a converted trawler which was part of the RN Patrol Service, mostly involved in renewing and repairing boom defences. 'One evening our crew were at the cinema when a message appeared on screen: "All Norina crew members to muster on jetty immediately". A convoy somewhere off Coll had been bombed with two vessels sunk and one badly damaged, which was struggling through the Sound of Mull in an effort to make Oban. She was being pursued by a German aircraft harassing her with machine gun fire. We met up with her in darkness and became a target ourselves – it was the first time we had been under fire. We simply aimed at the planes exhaust and fired – we only had Lewis machine guns. On another occasion at the cinema a message went up simply asking for volunteers. On this occasion a merchant ship was steaming down the Sound of Mull having suffered bomb damage.

Chariot (Human Torpedo) crewman being helped aboard a depot ship. Michael Groombridge remembers Loch Corrie being busy with Combined Operations canoeists and raiding parties preparing for D-Day while he and other 'midget' men practised oxygen dives 'among the octopuses'. (Morrison)

The problem was she was carrying an unexploded bomb in one of her coal bunkers. Royal Navy volunteers were asked to tow her back to the Firth of Lorne and help in the recovery of the bomb. After both of these escapades, our reward was free entry to the cinema next night.'

One man who visited most north-west coast ports in wartime during his service with the RN Patrol Service was Frank Bentley. 'From 1943 until 1946 I served aboard a converted trawler *Walwyns Castle*, one of a flotilla of similar ships pressed into war service as minesweepers. Most of the crews were naval reservists from the fishing fleets of the UK. I was the ship's gun layer. Our flotilla was based at various times at Stornoway, Loch Ewe and the Kyle of Lochalsh. The Navy's presence on Scotland's north-west coast was of great importance.

'At the convoy base at Loch Ewe ships gathered for the Russian run and the North Atlantic convoys. Kyle of Lochalsh was a mine laying base, and later a minesweeping base. Ships came and went from these places using the "War Channel" – that is from the Clyde through the Minches beyond Cape Wrath and the Butt of Lewis.

'We swept for five days then spent two days in base for refuelling etcetera. Towards the end of the war our flotilla was moved to Kyle of Lochalsh (HMS *Trelawney*), which was remote and ideal for hiding a large number of ships. At the entrance there was an anti-submarine gate which was opened and closed by a boom defence ship. On the cliff at the eastern end of the loch was the port war signal station, operated entirely by a small detachment of Wrens. The Loch Alsh Hotel, formerly the Railway Hotel, was the HQ of the base. Kyle was quite small, and had no electricity until the Navy arrived with its own generators. The Navy organised all the entertainment in the village. Only one piano was available, and this was moved around the village as necessary.

'A large hutted base at Aultbea, Loch Ewe, controlled the mustering of convoy ships either Atlantic, Arctic or Russia

Royal Navy and Royal Marines at their camp at Gallanach. (Bond)

A Motor Launch struggling up the Sound of Mull – the reality of life at sea off Scotland's West Coast. (McDonald)

Loch Ewe, an important gathering point for convoys, in wartime. One of the most significant events here during the war occurred on 27 February 1944 when the William H Welch, *a Liberty ship, was dashed onto rocks at Loch Ewe in a dreadful storm. Sixty US seamen lost their lives though locals managed to save quite a few sailors.* (National Maritime Museum Greenwich)

bound. The loch could accommodate the largest ships, naval or mercantile. Indeed one large warship, HMS *Nelson*, struck a mine when approaching the entrance in the early days of the war. She survived to fight another day.

'At the end of the war the German U-boat fleet was ordered to surface and be escorted by RN ships. Some crews were taken to Kyle of Lochalsh for transfer by train to prisoner of war camps. Perhaps fitting that the end of their war was on our patch from where so many merchant ships departed, some for their last voyage'.

There were many other ships belonging to the Royal Naval Patrol Service in and around west coast waters. Selby Middleton and Ieaun Timothy were on board HMS *Wolves* a 'Football Class' converted trawler. It would accompany the lighthouse boat on their duties and had to meet convoys and sometimes pick up bodies of dead seamen for burial at Oban. They played football ashore at Oban wearing strips donated by Wolverhampton Wanderers FC.

Midget Submarines

After suffering a number of setbacks at the hands of Italian midget subs, Churchill decided it was time to take this means of making war seriously. The west coast of Scotland proved the ideal location for top secret trials with firstly 'Chariots', a two-man torpedo-like craft which had a detachable warhead, and then 'X-craft', a midget submarine carrying a crew of four. Through the use of these two Britain was able to inflict some devastating blows, not least being the disabling of Germany's largest battleship, the *Tirpitz*, in September 1943. The damage was such that it took six months to repair her, and she was repeatedly attacked by the RAF and Fleet Air Arm and sunk in November 1944.

The 12th Submarine Flotilla's home during the war was at Port Bannatyne on the Isle of Bute in the Clyde, although

X-craft on surface patrol. (Morrison)

regular use was made of Loch Linnhe, Loch Corrie, Loch Eriboll and Loch Cairnbawn as exercise areas. The depot's ships were *Titania* and *Bonaventure*.

Among those who trained in this part of the world with the midget submarines were Robert Aitken DSO, who was captured during the *Tirpitz* raid, and Ian Fraser VC, who spent time at Loch Corrie preparing for his eventual X-craft mission against the Japanese. As a nineteen-year-old midshipman Robert Aitken volunteered for 'special duties', not knowing what lay ahead. He practised in Loch Corrie sitting astride Chariots, cutting wire nets to simulate breaking enemy defences. He transferred to X-craft and in September 1943 was in one of the 'Tirpitz' crews. Aitken was in X7 which was badly damaged by its own explosive

A typical convoy ship crammed with supplies, as seen by one of her RAF escorts. (Weatherall)

charges. He was trapped aboard over two hours below the *Tirpitz* with dead crewmates before escaping with only seconds of oxygen left and being captured.

Another visitor to Loch Corrie was the 'Sleeping Beauty', a semi-submersible canoe propelled by an electric motor. These were only used in action once – the mission had to be aborted and all the commandos involved were captured by the Japanese and executed.

Convoys

It is estimated that over 30,000 Allied merchant seamen died during World War Two in what was the least publicised of the services. For them there was no time limit to

their tour of duty, and when they were sunk or had no ship, they were not paid until another voyage began. Some merchant ships which were used during the war were old, slow and low on comfort, and convoys often had to proceed at the speed of the slowest member. Some vessels were crammed to bursting point with every conceivable cargo to help Britain avoid starvation.

It was the role of Royal Naval bases like Oban to escort the convoys coming in and out of the U-boat-infested waters off Scotland's north-west coast. Ron Blaber was a gun layer on a destroyer, HMS *Sturdy*, in 1940, when the Royal Navy was really struggling to come to terms with the Battle of the Atlantic. He found himself at a Hebridean island in unexpected and sad circumstances. 'Our work consisted of looking after outward bound convoys for about three days, then picking up homeward bound ones. Our outward convoy went smoothly and the first night after collecting our homeward ships everything seemed peaceful with no hint of danger, then without warning we lost eleven ships in ten minutes. There was simply nothing we could do, no sign of targets to attack.

'We arrived back at base for two days' rest, then we took out another convoy. All went well except for the weather, which slowly but surely deteriorated. When we came to make our turn around there was no sign of the homeward convoy, so we made our way eastward with the force of the storm on our tail. It was pretty rough for some of the young lads, being their first experience of life at sea.

'Just as I came off middle watch there was a loud roaring, ripping sound and the ship came to a sudden stop, with a great hissing of steam. At first I thought we had been hit by a torpedo but soon realised that the ship was sitting astride a reef and being lifted up and down with great jerks – no doubt why it finally broke in two.

'I volunteered to try to get a rope ashore. I was lowered to the sea with three others to a Carley float. An enormous

A dramatic sequence of photographs showing the end of the Geraldine Mary, *a 7000-ton merchant ship torpedoed by a U-boat on 4 August 1940. The photographs were taken from a Sunderland flying from Oban.* (Goddard, RAAF)

wave picked us up and tossed us over the rocks. Unfortunately the rope was covered with oil and could not be held. There was no way of getting back over the rocks to retrieve it so we made our way inland to seek help. We found some crofts, discovered we were on Tiree, and tried to signal to our ship by torch. However, they had seen us vanish in a cloud and decided to try using the ship's whaler. Given the rocks ahead it was a fatal mistake which cost the lives of five men as their boat was dashed on the rocks.

'The whole of the following week we stayed on the island, billeted in local homes. The main body of men were sent

Ron Blaber's ship, HMS Sturdy, *which ran aground on Tiree on 28 October 1940 near Sandaig on Tiree.* (Maclean)

Atlantic. During May 1943 no fewer than forty U-boats were sunk.'

John MacLean was, in 1941, a message boy in Boots the Chemist in Argyll Square, Oban. 'I saw a Merchant Navy skipper going into the shipping office on the North Pier and asked if he needed any crew. He said with my parents' permission I could join. So I joined MV *Hope Range*, a 5000-ton cargo vessel, as a deck boy. When I told my father he then joined up with another vessel in the Firth of Lorne, SS *Hindpool*, a tramp steamer. I left next morning for West Africa in convoy, but I never saw my father again – his ship was torpedoed.'

back to Portsmouth. My job was to strip down the guns and get them ashore, and also to remove and make safe the ammunition. I have been back to look at the lads' graves. It was a lovely sunny day and it all looked so peaceful, so unlike that fateful morning.'

Tom Birch was a radar operator and quartermaster/helmsman on board *Northern Spray*, an anti-submarine trawler which worked up at Tobermory in late 1942. 'We took part in the convoy ONS5 as part of the escort group B7. We assembled off Islay and sailed into the Atlantic on 23 April 1943. Almost immediately we were picked up by a U-boat pack and then shadowed by various packs throughout the entire journey. This was a ten-day-long battle over 1000 miles of sea. Twelve merchant ships were lost but eight U-boats were sunk. At the height of the battle *Northern Spray* had picked up no fewer than 145 survivors of various nationalities from sunken ships. However, ONS5 was later regarded as the turning point in the Battle of the

MTB crewmen who were based at Fort William and Oban. (Courteney)

Motor Gun Boats coming down Loch Linnhe. Many crews trained at Fort William for operations which included the raid on St Nazaire. MLs from Oban and Fort William patrolled the Firth of Lorne keeping ASDIC watch to Islay and beyond. Four MLs at Tobermory patrolled to the Western Isles and watch was kept on the few fishing boats that operated off these areas, as well as small ferry boats supplying the islands. (Cockburn)

On 2 October 1942, the anti-aircraft cruiser *Curacao* was escorting the huge liner *Queen Mary* off the north-west coast of Ireland. The *Queen Mary* was carrying 15000 US troops bound for the Clyde and *Curacao* was zig-zagging in front of her guarding against U-boats when the *Queen Mary* sliced *Curacao* completely in two, carrying part of the stricken cruiser on her bows a considerable way. Well over 300 sailors lost their lives. Though this incident was witnessed by many on board the *Queen Mary* it was hushed up until the end of the war for fear of the effect on morale.

Some of these sailors' graves can be seen at Pennyfuir cemetery, Oban.

Fort William

Fort William was home to a training base for MTB (Motor Torpedo Boat) and ML (Motor Launch) officers and crews. The Highland and Waverley hotels were taken over as the establishment of HMS *St Christopher* was built up. Training here was extensive and many crews went on to illustrious

Dunstaffnage camp and pier, built by Royal Marine Engineers. (Dunbeg School)

service such as in the raid on St Nazaire in March 1942 when the RN and a force of Commandos made a daring attack on the huge Nazi battleship *Tirpitz* and the only dry dock on France's Atlantic coast. Three out of four of the Allied servicemen involved were killed or became POWs and five VCs were awarded. The aluminium works in the area were the subject of Luftwaffe attacks, but they did not suffer serious damage. As with elsewhere the nature of the Highland terrain proved superb for other military training with one notable example being the commandos at Achnacarry.

Duncan Campbell was at HMS *St Christopher*. 'Motor Launches provided escorts for coastal convoys, carried out rescue operations, mine sweeping, escorted landing craft into attack and various other clandestine operations. Patrols were very important in the west coast area of Scotland as German submarines would go to any lengths to obtain success.'

Dunstaffnage

As Oban RN Base was declining in size and numbers by 1943, a base for a floating dock built by Royal Marine Engineers was opening at nearby Dunstaffnage (now Dunbeg). Admiralty Floating Dock XIX arrived at Dunstaffnage on 30 November 1942 having suffered a Luftwaffe attack on the way up from Portsmouth. There was, for a time, another floating dock at Corpach.

The first ship to dock at Dunstaffnage was HMS *Cygnet* in September 1943. Most refits were for five or six weeks duration. Herbert Saunders was stationed at Dunstaffnage Camp from June 1943 until March 1944 with the Royal Marines. 'We built a floating dock base for servicing ships and submarines of the Atlantic Fleet. It was an ideal spot – a secluded deep water inlet with the railway nearby. In the event of an air raid the dock could be completely submerged and remain invisible until the all clear.

'I was transferred to an assault landing craft. We trained hard around the island of Mull, practising landing on the beaches by day and night along with the Royal Marine Commandos. This was in the February, March and April of 1944. Little did we realise then that all this training was in preparation for the invasion of Europe on 6 June.

'Life was austere at Dunstaffnage and discipline was very harsh and strict. We had to wash our clothes in a bucket, but we managed to keep up a smart appearance so that we were presentable when we went into Oban. I enjoyed the most fabulous Xmas and Hogmanay of my life put on by the WAAFs at Ganavan.'

Edward Smith also recalls this base. 'I volunteered for service with the Royal Marines and came to Oban/Dunstaffnage in August 1942. We would march to Taynuilt

A fairly unassuming family snap which is one of the very few photographic records of the floating dock (top right) hidden in Dunstaffnage Bay. (McCulloch)

DUNSTAFFNAGE VILLAGE, NEAR OBAN   B 5394

Accommodation at Dunstaffnage built for floating dock workers from Admiralty bases in southern England who moved north with their families. (McCulloch)

or over Connel Bridge with mock battles to hold the bridge against "enemy" forces using blank ammunition, smoke bombs etcetera. On one occasion, under supervision, we used live ammunition.'

Bob Blatchford was part of the group of dock workers who came north from Portsmouth. They included ship-wrights, fitter turners, coppersmiths, boilermakers, joiners, painters and drawing office staff. The working area was supervised by Metropolitan policemen. 'Pinnaces ferried workers and materials to the dock. Living quarters for the workers were one and two bedroom prefabricated houses. There were around 250 families living in these houses. Single men lived in a hostel in Oban. We had a general store, run by the Co-op, and a Nissen hut cinema which was also used as a Sunday school. Dances were held when ships' crews came ashore.

'Near the time for the second front we converted small vessels into landing craft. We converted about forty craft for this purpose.

'The floating dock could take destroyers, corvettes and ships up to around 18,000 tons. When the ships were positioned and secured by timbers the water was pumped out making it a dry dock. We had American, Canadian and at least three Russian ships call in for repairs.'

Stella (Martin) Taylor was a schoolgirl during the war. 'When my father had to move up to Dunstaffnage from Portsmouth dock yard, my mother, brother and I came with him to live. We were in a flat-roofed, prefab building. We had to go to school in Oban and I remember knuckles were rapped with a ruler if we couldn't pronounce the poems or language of Robert Burns properly. We also had to learn verses from the Bible.'

Patricia (Millman) Palmer was another youngster who came north. 'I managed to find a job as a post woman taking telegrams to local farms and cottages. I was paid by the miles I walked. When American ships visited the floating dock they used to hand out chewing gum, chocolates and nylon stockings.'

Peter Wood came to Dunstaffnage in April 1944 as a watchkeeping seaman. 'My ship was sent to Dunstaffnage for a major refit and rearmament for the impending D-Day attacks. Imagine our amazement to see, near Connel Bridge, a big floating dock. After the refit came the toughening up process which was laid on for us at nearby Tobermory. This consisted of a series of "action stations" situations. Fires were actually set in various parts of the ship and we came under attack from our own fighter aircraft firing live ammunition. After this we chased submarines around the Western Isles. Next came Channel convoys and of course D-Day.'

The last vessel to refit at Dunstaffnage, HMS *Inver*, left on 2 June 1945 and the floating dock was towed to the Clyde and then to the Far East departing 15 July 1945.

3

Commonwealth Comrades in Arms

WITH BOTH an RAF and RN presence in Oban in the years 1939 to 1945, the town was always a busy, active place. Distinctive amongst the bustle and adding to the cosmopolitan flavour of the times was a significant representation of servicemen from overseas, notably Australia and Canada, but also some from the USA, France, New Zealand and even a Fijian. Their contribution to the Battle of the Atlantic was a notable one and is remembered with pride by both locals and the men themselves.

People arrived from the world over to join the fight around the UK shores. This desire to contribute is well demonstrated by Giff Blamey, who volunteered for the RNZAF and set sail from New Zealand in December 1940 via the Panama Canal and the frozen North Atlantic. He and his fellow volunteers flooded up on deck and cheered at the first sight through the mist of Butt of Lewis Lighthouse. They had travelled half way round the world on cargo ships loaded with food.

Australians

10 Squadron RAAF (Royal Australian Air Force) found themselves in the UK in September 1939, carrying out trials on Sunderland flying boats. The British Government requested they be allowed to remain after the outbreak of hostilities, and so they became the first operational Australian Squadron of the war. The Squadron's Sunderlands arrived at Oban in July 1940 and detachments operated from this base until April 1941, during which time they played a big part in guarding the North Western approaches.

One of the first RAAF men to reach Oban was Bill Vout. 'On the 30 July 1940 I was a crew member (First Engineer) on board a Sunderland which took off from Mountbatten, Plymouth, bound for Oban. We weren't sorry to leave Plymouth for a spell as we had been subjected to some pretty heavy air raids. There was some speculation at the time that German U-boats were using Irish ports for provisioning so we were ordered to travel around the Irish

RAAF pilot standing on a Sunderland with Oban in the background. (Burrage)

south and west coasts as closely as politically legal. However, we saw no sign of U-boat activity. Next day we did a twelve-hour patrol escorting a tremendous convoy with ships seeming to stretch from horizon to horizon.

'We experienced one very sad occasion during this tour of duty. An RAF Sunderland returning from patrol attempted a landing in the Firth during thick fog but crashed. I remember standing helplessly by the railings on the seafront along Corran Esplanade, listening to the survivors' cries for help. Boats from the marine section were desperately trying to locate the men in the fog. To add to their problems a pinnace carrying a doctor ran aground on Kerrera.'

Flight Lieutenant (Later Air Commodore) Reg Burrage OBE DFC MID, was a pilot with 10 Squadron. 'After a walk around Oban I noted in my diary that "The country is undoubtedly the prettiest we have seen since setting foot in the UK. We passed by many beautiful lochs and through several deep glens. Waterfalls enhanced the grandness of the russet tinted mountains."

'On 16 November I experienced my first operational mission from Oban, which was to make a marked impression on me. Seeking to rendezvous with a convoy approximately 300 nautical miles west of Ireland, we came across an unescorted British merchant vessel SS *Planter*. As we circled low some of the ship's crew members stood in line across the front of the bridge and waved a cheery greeting. We waggled our wings in acknowledgement but had no option but to continue on course.

'Following our return to Oban we heard that SS *Planter* had been torpedoed and sunk. I could not remove from my mind the thought of the crew standing on the bridge and waving so cheerfully. That image still haunts me to this day.'

Keith Phillips, a Corporal with 10 Squadron in 1940, asked his family to keep his letters home during the war

Australian airmen relaxing on Oban golf course. (Burrage)

Basil Thornton of 10 Squadron RAAF at his gun position on a Mark I Sunderland. (Thornton)

as a record of his time in the RAAF, including service at Oban.

'2 Sept 1940: Have been standing by for several days to proceed to the west coast of Scotland. They say it's as cold as charity up there now.

10 Sept 1940: Am writing this on watch at the signals desk on a sub-hunt over the North Atlantic. We are operating from Oban and it really is as cold as charity. The town is very pretty in a lovely setting, but it is a foul place to fly in.

11 Sept: I turned in at 11 last night after a bath, expecting to go aboard about 8 a.m. but a couple of ships got torpedoed about 3 a.m. so we were routed out at 4 a.m. to hunt for the sub. Dawn is just breaking and we are scooting along the north coast of Ireland. Just found one of the torpedoed ships still afloat with her stern blown off from the aft hatch to the rudder. Two naval ships are coming up over the horizon, so going off sub-hunting now. I'll bet the cows are sound asleep below the surface and won't come up again till dusk.

12–16 Sept: They are shoving the work into us and we haven't had a chance to get near a shop or a post office for nearly a week.

17 Sept: Had half a day off today – must be the end of the war! Last night was the first for a week that we were not called at 4 a.m. and then they woke us at 5 a.m. for an air raid warning. Some of the boys are billeted in private homes where they are well looked after but we have had no such luck.

30 Sept: We flew 105 hours in 18 days.

5 Oct: The weather closed in suddenly, landed at Lochboisdale. It was raining like Hades and blowing all-out and getting dark. In the morning everything was calm and peaceful and looking as if butter wouldn't melt on it – and neither it would it was too damn cold.

15 Oct: Left Oban.'

In September 1940 the liner *City of Benares* was sunk with the loss of almost 300 people, including 80 children who were being evacuated to Canada. The loss was the cause of great national grief, keenly felt in places like Oban. Stan Goddard, a navigator with 10 Squadron, remembers a patrol not long afterwards. 'On 25 September 1940 our

Survivors from the SS Stan Grant *disembarking from the Sunderland flown by Vic Hodgkinson of 10 Squadron which had landed in the Atlantic to pick them up. Twenty-one men had been adrift for over a week after their ship had been sunk.* (Hodgkinson)

Stan Goddard of 10 Squadron RAAF at his navigator's table. He spotted the survivors of the City of Benares.

Flying boat 'RB-B', like the Sunderland on which Stan Goddard and crew were flying when they spotted the City of Benares' *survivors.* (Burrage)

Sunderland departed Oban to rendevous with a convoy. On our return flight to Oban we sighted a lifeboat with sails set. As we came closer we saw that the boat was full of people. Standing on a seat amidship was a boy in a Scout uniform waving his arms. We realised that he was signalling in semaphore and we read "City of Benares". Naturally we were overjoyed because it was eight days since the ship was torpedoed and there had been little hope of finding further survivors.

'Our captain tried on three occasions to alight on the choppy sea. We could not so we dropped supplies wrapped in "Mae Wests" [lifebelts] with a smoke float. We were running low on fuel but found another Sunderland and RN escort vessel who picked up the survivors. We arrived back at Oban after being airborne for 13 hours 45 minutes and with almost no petrol left – but it was worth it. What a night in the Alexandra Hotel! I wasn't allowed to buy a drink.' [The lifeboat contained more than 30 survivors including 6 children.]

Canadians

423 Squadron RCAF (Royal Canadian Air Force) was formed at Oban on 18 May 1942 and remained at Oban until November 1942. Another Canadian squadron, 422, were also at Oban from May 1943 until November 1943. Both squadrons flew Sunderlands, although 422 had some Catalinas at first. Many men of 413 Squadron RCAF also 'worked up' at the Ferry Training Unit at Oban.

Lloyd Jamieson, RCAF, was very pleased to be posted in Scotland. 'My mother was born and raised in Glasgow and the family emigrated to Canada about 1910. Oban was a welcome posting. One thing I remember very well is the vacation train from Glasgow arrived every weekend and

Fl/Lt Sid Butler DFC (third right) and his Canadian crew on their Sunderland with Dunollie Castle in the background, 1943. (Butler)

there were many nice young ladies aboard and we went to dances, concerts and movies.'

Eric Middleton, RCAF, wrote: 'One thing is quite beyond doubt, Oban was the best station of my service life. It was so good to be in a town. I found it such a pleasure to be able to just pop out of the "billet" and be in a civilian community and I enjoyed strolling around the town – and the occasional coffee at Kennedy's cafe.'

Jack Scannell was an Irishman living in England who volunteered and joined the Royal Canadian Air Force. 'The staff in one Oban pub taught me some of the Gaelic which they spoke and I was able to pick it up quite quickly as I spoke the Irish Gaelic. They took me to see shinty games and I joined in some as I played hurling as a youth in

Ireland. It was in Oban that I got my first taste for golf as we were loaned clubs and balls and given free access to the course. I am still hooked on it.'

Bill Stevenson was an RAF man working alongside the RCAF at Oban. He remembers two Canadians in particular who made an impact. 'Terrence Rattigan was an air gunner commissioned with the RCAF. He was a very quiet, polite man, who spent his off-duty time writing in his room at the Esplanade Hotel. The name didn't mean much at the time, but I read many years later that he wrote his hit play *Flare Path* during that time.

'"Tiny" Hunter was a giant of a man at 6 feet 9 inches with breadth to match. He'd been the heavyweight champion of the London Metropolitan Police. He had just come off operational flying for a bit, and had a DFC then, and was serving with 423 RCAF at Oban.'

Don Wells was a Canadian pilot who first flew in a Sunderland from Oban and was astonished at the contrast in scenery with his home in the flatlands of Canada. He married a WAAF he met at Oban and after the war they met an Oban man in Canada. He had owned the Marine Hotel in Oban which was commandeered and became the RAF Sergeants' mess. When this man was called up for the RAF at a rank below Sergeant he returned to the hotel to retrieve some belongings he had locked away. He was promptly arrested by RAF policemen who refused to accept his story for quite some time.

4

Oban RAF Training Base, 1943–1945

IN THE EARLY PART of the war, the pre-eminence of flying boats represented the RAF's main counter to the U-boat, and Oban's main role was as an operational base. However, as the war progressed technological advances led to land-based aircraft becoming more effective, so landing strips at places such as Tiree and Benbecula evolved as the main operational bases and Oban's role centred more on logistical and communication support. It was also used as a training base, and from July 1943 until 1945 RAF Oban was the home of 302 FTU (Ferry Training Unit). Catalina and Sunderland crews completed their training here and were allocated their own flying boat prior to posting to an operational unit. As the Battle of the Atlantic gradually decreased and the U-boats were nearing defeat, attention turned to the war in the Far East, and RAF crews would leave Oban for exotic sounding destinations such as Apapa (West Africa), Batavia (Java), Koggala (Ceylon) and Seletar (Singapore).

As Oban became more crowded than ever with training airmen and support staff, satellite bases at Connel and Ganavan were incorporated into the main RAF station. From October to December 1943, 524 Squadron was at Oban to trial the American Martin Mariner flying boat. However the RAF eventually decided to return these aircraft to the USA as they were deemed unsuitable at the time.

Many memories of Oban flying boat base centre around tragic events. Ron Anstey was a Sergeant Wireless Operator/Air Gunner: 'My first Captain at Oban was Flight Sergeant David Clyne. He was a Glaswegian and the Queen's Park soccer captain who had captained Scotland as an amateur. The second pilot Eddie Kilshaw was also an excellent footballer, a professional who played for Bury in the English league. In fact we had a very good station football team, which included Dave Johnston, a Hearts centre-forward.

'We were involved in a crash on the night of 12 May 1944 when carrying a full fuel load and depth charges under

A three-shot sequence showing a Sunderland at Oban turning to begin its take-off run, during the take-off run across the Firth of Lorne and 'on the step', about to take off. (Stevenson)

A Martin Mariner flying boat of 524 Squadron, which came to Oban in 1943, taxiing in the Firth of Lorne. Note the distinctive gull wings. (Southwell)

(Top right) A Sunderland returning to the Scottish coast in winter after a mission. Among the duties performed by 302 FTU was dropping food supplies to Hebridean islands when ferries could not get through in storms, assisting in trials with midget submarines in Loch Corrie and carrying commandos and their canoes to remote lochs and glens for practice sabotage exercises. (Wilson)

each wing. Our Catalina failed to clear high ground on Vatersay Island and crashed into a hillside. Dave Clyne, Fred Bassett, a WOP/AG and Patrick Hine (the Rigger) were killed. The other six of us escaped. Roy Beavis, the engineer, was the only conscious crew member after the crash and managed to put out a fire which had started in the engine nacelles (housing) by throwing clumps of earth on it. He also obtained help in the morning from a croft down below. We survivors were taken to Barra by the Navy and then to the Cottage Hospital in Oban.'

One remarkable act of bravery long remembered by those at Oban at the time was carried out by Corporal Fred Styles, an ASR coxswain. On 7 November 1943 a Catalina coming in from patrol landed badly, bounced, flipped over and began to sink. Despite orders to the contrary. Styles dived in to the freezing water, swam to the Catalina and got in via a blister window. He rescued three unconscious airmen by pulling them free and swimming to the ASR launch. In his attempts to free others he even tied a rope to the

RAF Marine Craft Unit men at Dungallan Pier. (Ward)

Catalina's tail and tried to have it towed to Oban pier. The rope snapped and the flying boat sank. Styles was awarded the BEM by the King at Holyrood. One of the crew on Styles' rescue launch that night was Fred Luke who won the VC in World War One serving in the Royal Artillery.

A Catalina on night patrol. The Catalina could undertake very long-range patrols and was particularly suited to operations carried out deep into enemy-held territory. (Williams)

Bill Stevenson was ground crew at Oban during 1942 and 1943. 'I played in one football game, Oban select versus Services select. Oban beat us 14–1, which wasn't bad for a team that was only supposed to be good at shinty. Also, dances were held regularly in the NAAFI canteen which was in the Park Hotel dining room. There was an excellent station dance band, made up of five professional musicians who had been members of the famous "Snake Hips" Johnson's Dance Band.' Tony Sloe was a famous cartoonist in magazines pre-war who had also painted scenery for the film industry. At Oban he was an RAF coxswain on Marine craft. He painted many cartoons of airmen and WAAFS on the walls of the Park Hotel.

In general, most of the men who served in the later years of the war have pleasant memories of their posting. Reg Moorwood, a Wireless Operator with 302 FTU, was posted to Oban in August 1944. 'I think I was the oldest but one of the crew, at the ripe old age of twenty-two. We were in

Fred Styles standing on top of the Park Hotel, Oban, after receiving the BEM for bravery. (Styles)

Wings for Victory dance alongside Columba Hotel, North Pier, Oban, 1943. Such events were evidence for many of the servicemen and women in Oban that things were getting a little bit better. (Jones)

(Right) Sunderland of 330 Squadron (Norwegian) being repaired at Ganavan, Oban. (Steffen-Olsen)

no hurry to leave Oban – I didn't really think I would ever return.

'As the time to depart approached a number of snags kept surfacing with the flying boat, which perhaps wasn't surprising as Oban in early August was a beautiful place, and the future prospect for us was tropical heat, a foreign country, and the possibility of fairly close contact with very unfriendly Japs, who were still uncomfortably close to the Indian border.' [Moorwood was in fact badly injured on the journey out to Karachi when his Catalina crashed.]

302 FTU made extensive use of the facilities at Ganavan Sands, to the north-west of Oban. Corporal Andy Andrews remembers: 'As Ganavan was about two miles from Oban and only a small unit, a group of us applied for and were granted permission to hold dances on Sunday nights. There had been dances before we arrived, but not with transport.

Until then girls were ferried back and forth on the crossbar of their partner's bike, a painful journey no doubt.

'Although the dances were held on a Sunday, airmen were still expected to be available twenty-four hours per day. To this end duty crews were organised and would be made to dress in accordance with orders, i.e. rubber boots, overalls and thick white roll neck pullovers. They would be working if required, hauling wet ropes and fitting trolleys under Sunderland aircraft prior to dragging them out of the water. On one or two occasions, the crew men would pop in and sneak a beer, and the girls in their fancy dresses were asked to help pulling ashore a Sunderland which they did, manfully and wonderfully.'

Norman Holdsworth remembers: 'We usually got as many people as possible together to pull flying boats up the slipway. On one occasion an engineering officer decided to try pulling a Catalina up the slipway using a long cable running through a pulley at the top of the slipway. With the aircraft near the top of the slip the pulley broke. Fortunately the aircraft went straight down the slipway back into the sea, although the cable whizzed across and broke a WAAF's leg. End of experiment!'

Ken Stoker was part of the large Marine Craft Unit/Air Sea Rescue presence at Oban. 'In 1944 I was in the Marine Craft Unit and was in charge of a twenty-four-foot launch. I was eighteen years of age. Among the vessels we had were refuelling boats, bomb scows, fire tenders, flying control pinnaces and seaplane tenders. We ferried back and forth to Kerrera and Ganavan.

'My time at Oban came to a rather abrupt end. The CO told us that Sholto-Douglas, Officer Commanding, RAF Coastal Command would visit Oban towards the end of 1944. We were ordered to scrub and polish everything at Kerrera. When Sholto-Douglas inspected he decided that as the base looked so good we must have had too much time on our hands. Forty men were posted overseas. I was one of them.'

Another RAF establishment close to Oban was situated at Connel, north of Loch Etive. The Air Ministry planned and built a forward fighter aerodrome in 1941, but RAF Connel was never fully in use as an operational base. It

Ganavan Sands, Oban, in 1946, with the large RAF hangar and Nissen huts still in place. (Budge)

was mainly utilised as an Emergency Landing Ground (ELG) and as an Air Ammunition Park. Connel had at different times a variety of roles in support of nearby RAF Oban. There was a radio station, WAAF site (south of the Falls of Lora), a holding camp for air crews with many Nissen huts and training classrooms. It was also frequently used for emergency landings by RAF, USAAF (United States Army Air Force) and FAA (Fleet Air Arm) aircraft.

516 combined Operational Squadron made use of Connel in early 1944 for exercises, a period which was marred by the loss of three Hurricanes which had arrived at the base on detachment. Of the three planes which left for an exercise at Kentra Bay, Ardnamurchan, on 6 February 1944, one made a successful crash landing in a field near Stirling, one pilot was killed on the Isle of Coll and the other died in a crash near Ardnamurchan Point.

A Halifax of 518 Squadron taking off on a met flight from Tiree. Ben Hough and the radar unit (to the left, above the beach) are visible. (Campbell/Diamond)

TIREE AIRSTRIP, known by all as 'the Reef', was originally requisitioned for work to begin preparing a major airfield at the height of the invasion fears in August 1940. A grass airstrip had been operated on the Reef by Scottish Airways since 1934. Many European countries fell to the Nazis in 1940. Convoys were re-routed from the English Channel and North Sea to the west coast of Scotland and Northern Ireland. RAF Tiree was formally opened as part of 15 Group, RAF Coastal Command on 28 November 1941. No. 31 [EU] Embarkation Unit RAF was stationed at Tiree from April 1941, and remained on the island until disbanding on 31 December 1945.

The first fully operational squadron, 224, arrived on 8 April 1942. They flew Hudsons and carried out anti-submarine sweeps and air/sea rescue sorties over the Atlantic. In July the squadron began converting to Liberators and on 9 September 1942 they left Tiree. Meanwhile, during May and June of the same year, 304 (Polish) Squadron, equipped with Wellingtons, was based at Tiree. When they left the Station moved on to a 'care and maintenance' basis until the arrival of 518 (Meteorological Reconnaissance) Squadron on 24 September 1943. Equipped with Halifax aircraft, the Squadron's main task was gathering weather information. 518 Squadron remained at Tiree until 18 September 1945. In addition, during 1944/45, 281 ASR Squadron (and a detachment of 280 Squadron) operated from Tiree with Warwick aircraft.

During 1940 a radio unit was established at Scarinish. At this time the duties of the RAF men stationed on the island included maintaining the Post Office Repeater Station while

the EU assisted with the building of the drome and all transport including towing away crashed aircraft from around the island and repairing ASR launches which spent time at Scarinish. Hugh Hunter was one of the first to arrive on radar work. 'I was one of the initial airmen sent to Tiree to Port Mor in 1941, where a few stayed in a croft and others in a bell tent. We then moved to our permanent site at Kilkenneth. The RAF were advised against building on the site by locals and my Nissen hut had water from end to end for a short time – we had to step straight into wellingtons when rising.

The Lochearn, *a MacBraynes ferry/transport ship in Gott Bay, Tiree. These ferries were the main link for servicemen to Oban and the mainland.* (McKinnon)

A Nissen hut at the RAF Radar base at Kilkenneth on Tiree.

(Right) A Tiree woman using a butter plunger in front of her traditional thatched croft. This photograph was part of a series taken by George Holleyman, an RAF Policeman with an interest in archaeology and anthropology who was stationed on Tiree during 1942. (Holleyman)

'The early days on the island left much to be desired. We had no electric supply and we received paraffin for lamps about every four weeks but that only lasted about a week. Once there was a large lump of wax washed onto the beach and we used this to make our own candles. Our washing facilities were from tins filled with water from the streams and as cows often strolled into these ditches, it naturally had to be boiled before being used for cooking. The winds on occasion were hurricane force and our cookhouse was blown away with all the pots and pans etc. Initially I think the islanders were worried that when we arrived the war would be brought to their island, but as time progressed they forgot this and a very good relationship existed between us.'

Jack Liddy and Jim Fowler were among the men posted to the radar sites at Kilkenneth and Ben Hough in 1941. They found sites dispersed in three areas stretching from Barrapol to Balevulin. They faced a number of climbs up Ben Hough each day in all weathers. There a revolving aerial on mast had to be strapped down in gales. The unit included radar operators, mechanics, drivers, diesel engineers, cooks and a popular NAAFI. By good fortune they had a 'big name' in Freddie Holmes (of Radio Revellers fame) in the station dance band.

George Holleyman of the RAF Police also remembers the early days on the island. 'On September 27 1941 I was

The trawler, Ocean Tide, *which ran aground at Mannel, Tiree, in January 1942. The crew were rescued by the RAF under Wing Commander Tuttle, CO at Tiree.* (Holleyman)

posted to RAF Kilkenneth on the Isle of Tiree. I had a special reason for being somewhat excited at the prospect of visiting the Hebrides: from 1930 I had played an active role in archaeological excavation and anthropological research in Sussex. [In fact Holleyman discovered many artefacts during his time on Tiree which are now with the Sottish Museum of Antiquities.] I therefore procured a Gaelic grammar and reading book and with help from island friends I could read and write Gaelic reasonably well and could sing Gaelic songs and hymns.

'With a bicycle I was able to explore the whole island. Many of the townships were served only by very rough roads or just muddy and sandy tracks. Many of the airmen rarely left the station in their spare time but others got to know island families and received much true Highland hospitality. My estimate was that two thirds of the popu-

SS Ingrid, *a cargo vessel which ran aground near Cornaigmore, Tiree, January 1942.* (Holleyman)

304 (Polish) Squadron men take a break in front of a Wellington bomber undergoing servicing. (Ziomek)

'Waiting for the call.' Groundcrew of 304 Squadron await the return of aircraft. Among the ground crew with 304 were brothers Genek and Emil Ziomek. They came to Britain to continue the fight when Poland was overrun, and stayed as they had no home to return to after the war. (Ziomek)

Hudson of 224 Squadron over the Atlantic. A strong bond grew between 304 (Polish) Squadron and 224 Hudson Squadron when a Polish Wellington ditched during its first op and 224 Squadron all took off on a search which resulted in the full crew being rescued. (Frick)

An aerial shot from April 1942 showing the Tiree camp and airfield (the Reef) as it became operational. Note the scores of Nissen huts. (Clarke)

lation was still living in the traditional Hebridean thatched cottages, or similar cottages which had a bituminous roof of some sort. Nearly all the crofters' thatched houses had their barns and byres attached and sometimes a cart shed or fuel store might be added. At the time of my stay on the island the indigenous population was estimated at about 1450 but it was much enlarged by service personnel and labourers from the mainland. Oil lamps provided the

illumination, but hurricane lamps were handy if you wished to visit the byre or barn at night. Some crofts had earthen floors and furniture was made locally from drift-wood. Family income was derived mostly from the croft and a little fishing.

'My stay on Tiree coincided with the grimmest period of the Battle of the Atlantic when a huge tonnage of Allied merchant shipping was lost. The rocky headlands and sandy

Loading depth charges onto a Wellington of 304. (Solecki)

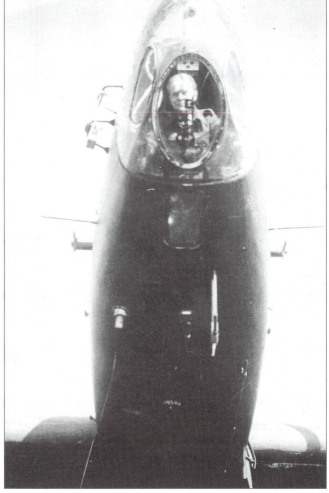

Halifax which overshot the runway at Tiree, 1945. During 518's time at Tiree there were no fewer than twelve crashes or loss of aircraft. (Pearman)

A Meteorological ('Met') Air Observer of 518 Squadron in the nose of a Halifax. (Faulkner)

bays of Tiree were strewn with flotsam and jetsam from this carnage.'

In 1942 304 (Polish) Squadron arrived at Tiree with only half its usual strength. They had suffered great losses while serving in Bomber Command over continental Europe, but

now had to get used to low-level bombing with Coastal Command. The Battle of the Atlantic was growing in intensity and U-boat detection was mostly by sight at the time.

518 (Meteorological Reconnaissance) Squadron arrived in September 1943, over a year after the departure of the Poles and 224 Squadron. Winston Diamond, an Australian navigator with 518, has written of the work of his Squadron. 'During our flights detailed information on the weather was sent back by wireless every half hour in meteorological code and wartime cypher. This was a vital ingredient in the forecasts upon which Allied military operations depended. Not only the planning of Bomber Command raids on German targets but the very date of the D-Day landings in Normandy on 6 June 1944 was determined by information supplied by the met squadrons.

'A ten-and-a-half hour trip was normal. Our purpose was to obtain barometric pressure, temperature and humidity readings plus weather, cloud and wind velocity data. The

The wedding of Roy and Sheila Stevenson in July 1944. Sheila was a WAAF at Tiree. Roy and all but one of his crew photographed here died when the two Halifaxes collided in August 1944. (Pelling)

The funeral of the airmen killed in the collision of two Halifaxes over Tiree airfield in August 1944. One man who died in this crash was Fl/Lt Len Revlliod, a nephew of Jan Masyrak and grandson of Thomas Mazaryk, the the first Prime Minister of Czechoslovakia. Jan Masyrak and Dr and Mrs Revlliod flew over to Tiree from their home in exile in London for the funeral. (Pelling)

flights were code named "Bismuth" or "Mercer". It was crucial that the pilot should fly the aircraft at exactly the right height and follow the other instructions given him by the met observer and the navigator. The navigation had to be spot-on, so that the readings taken by the met observer were correct. The flights had to be made, no matter what. During 1944 518 Squadron flew every single day but two. On one of these days our plane was scheduled to fly. It had snowed the day before and overnight the snow had frozen into ice. Three times we thundered down the runway only to skid off into the frozen grass. The trip was scrubbed.

'Wednesday 16 August was a black day for 518 Squadron. Halifaxes "M" and "S" were allowed off together to do an air test before the flight that night. This was the normal procedure but this particular day the cloud level was about 100ft. They took off and immediately were lost in the cloud. Shortly after there was a crash, then an almighty explosion and a burning wing fluttered to the ground just yards away from the Sergeants' Mess which had hundreds of men inside it at the time. The crews of both aircraft were all killed.

One 518 man, Ken Lunn, remembers the lighter side of island life. 'In September 1943, aged twenty, married eight

The Christmas party in the Sergeants' mess, RAF Tiree 1944. (Cobb)

weeks, I received a posting to Tiree. I could not find it on my road atlas. I found a room with a retired school teacher at a cottage in Balemartin for my wife and myself. It had an open fire, cooking water from a stream (by bucket) and a hole-in-the-ground toilet. A very religious lady, she blamed the aircraft for the poor crops and the bad weather.

'Another spare room was let out for a few days to an RAF Sergeant and his wife who was heavily pregnant. She decided to have a bath which was an old sink effort that used to hang on the wall. Water was heated on the open stove and eventually she got in. Trouble was she could not get out. Various ladies were called to assist but to no avail – her husband was on duty and it was explained to me that being a married man and having my wife present it was in order for me to assist in removing this female from the bath tub. Anyway the sight that met me when I entered the kitchen was something I shall never forget – I had to stand on the rim of the bath and push outward whilst the women present pulled her out by the feet. I still have nightmares thinking about it.'

Guy Pearman of 518 Squadron describes what the reality of an 'op' could be. 'At about 4.30 a.m. on 25 January 1945

A flight engineer at work in a Halifax. (Radford)

we were heading back to base with 300 miles to go when we flew into the back end of a cold front and were tossed about in thunder clouds. The whole aircraft and especially the propellers became bathed in St Elmo's fire. Suddenly, every member of the crew saw a brilliant flash in front of his eyes and then was out cold for several seconds. We had been struck by lightning. When I came to, I was sitting in an icy gale with my navigation log, maps and charts blown away. Most of the perspex nose had vanished. Ice started to form on the wings so we came down to about 200 feet, but still it formed, weighing the aircraft down. Suddenly the noise from the four Merlin engines died away – the carburettors had iced up. There was nothing for it but to wait for the end when the aircraft hit the sea. As we came

A lifeboat dropping from a 281 Squadron Warwick. These Lind-holme lifeboats had two small engines, a sail and lifelines which automatically fired out into the sea. The on-board provision included a radio, fishing gear, and glucose and benzedrine tablets. (Currie)

Members of 518 Squadron find something to enjoy in one of the worst snow storms ever to hit Tiree, January 1945. (Eastwood)

in to ditch the engines picked up again as suddenly as they had died. Slowly we climbed away from the sea. Half an hour later we landed safely at our Hebridean base escorted by the ASR (Air Sea Rescue) Warwick aircraft. Inspection of our aircraft after the flight revealed traces of seaweed on the tail-wheel!'

Flying Officer Pete Bridgewater remembers how close he came to death while with 518 on Tiree. 'I was lucky enough to be assigned to Flight Lieutenant Max Bacon's crew. He was the most experienced and most respected captain on the squadron, and his crew, with the obvious exception of myself, had been with him a long time and were as good as they get. I did about twenty operational trips as second pilot with that crew. One thing about the met flights was that you always went out, even if you knew that everywhere would be closed in when you got back you still took off. After landing at Tiree or elsewhere our crew had good times in the mess and we had money-makers in a champion darts player and a very fast beer drinker.

'The twenty-first trip that I was doing with Max was on 21 January 1945. We were doing "Bismuth" and FL/Lt "Archie" Archibald was doing "Mercer". It was not a nice night. Wing Commander Morris, the CO, decided to come with our crew. The Chief Met. Officer, FL/Lt Beutell, also joined Max's crew for the trip. We got to the end of the runway, with Archie's aircraft just behind us, and were halfway through the take-off check when Archie called up Max on the radio. He was very worried about being able to get safely through ten or eleven hours of this horrific weather with a second pilot who had never been on an operational flight before. Since I had done quite a few trips by then, would Max let the two second pilots change aircraft? After all, Max did have the Wing Commander to act as second pilot. Max and the Wing Co saw the sense of it and said yes, and I passed the new boy on the way across to change planes.

'We did have a hell of a trip. We had radio-altimeters, and they helped, but you could get 100 foot waves in the Atlantic, and you couldn't see them coming at night. When we neared home, we were told that Tiree was closed in, and we diverted to land at Turnberry. When we landed we were told that Max and crew had disappeared without trace. It was never known whether it was icing (January in that part of the Atlantic was very cold) or a large wave or some other problem.'

Many crews held their pilot in high esteem. The men who flew with 'three engine Butler', Les Cobb, Ken Harper (W/op AGs) and Ron Toy (navigator) all believe they owed their lives to Wilf Butler's skills as a pilot. Not just because they got back safely on three (once even two) engines from met flights, but also for other vital matters. For instance Butler once brought back thirty live turkeys in a plane from Northern Ireland for the station Christmas dinner!

18 Squadron was fortunate in the large numbers of dedicated Canadian and Australian aircrew who made up its numbers. Fl/Lt Doug Humphreys of RCAF was one of these. He and his fellow officers were not pleased about the living conditions of their non-commissioned crew members and they did not appreciate the RAF's class divisions. The food shocked them too: 'greyish bread, powdered milk, paper like cereal, pilchards with macaroni for dessert'.

Motor transport WAAF helping with repairs. In 1942, with more than 2000 RAF men stationed at Tiree, the first contingent of 40 WAAFS arrived. Some of them helped oversee the setting up of a WAAF code and cyphers section, while others did admin and work in the mess. There were also WAAFs for a time at the Fighter Operations Unit which was at Baugh on Tiree for a short period. From late 1943 onwards the number of WAAFs grew steadily. (Porazka)

Also part of the scene on Tiree were the WAAFs. They would work long shifts in the Ops block, in the parachute section, in the messes and many other roles. Many aquired bikes and toured and explored the island. Like the men they tried to obtain 'off-ration' eggs to send home. Georgie Porazka remembers after a plane crash the blood stained stretchers outside sick bay, while Elizabeth Lotocka arrived in 1945 with war coming to a close. After long hours driving lorries she swam at Balephuil or Balephetrish, with seals and the occasional sharks to be seen while sea birds dived for fish all around her.

Jim Ayers was at Tiree in 1945. 'Amongst my final duties with the RAF was assisting in the removal of RAF vehicles by landing craft from the beach at Gott Bay.' [Just as they had arrived in 1940.] Roy Smith was posted to Tiree after the war ended, as a storekeeper. 'I was part of a "care and maintenance party" as RAF Tiree was closing down and packing up. I was told that a lot of valuable and important equipment would be left behind because it was not practical to dismantle it, and (like us) it was surplus to requirements.'

A B17 Flying Fortress flies over a traditional croft on Benbecula 1943. This is an image of two very different cultures meeting in wartime. (Ayling 220 Squadron Association)

6

Benbecula

I N the 1930s Northern and Scottish Airways provided an air ambulance service to locations such as Barra and North and South Uist, with Suneval Strand on Benbecula coming into service latterly. Well-known captains such as Barclay and Fresson operated these runs in De Havilland Rapides with minimum or non-existent navigational equipment. Lochmaddy in North Uist, like many other Hebridean harbours, was also tried out by flying boats in the 1930s.

Early in 1939, as the war clouds were gathering, an RAF officer and a small group of airmen arrived to survey the Uists. At the parish hall in Griminish the news was broken to the islanders that Balivanich on Benbecula would have an RAF airfield. There was much trepidation among the crofters that the Gaelic culture might be under threat and land would have to be taken for RAF use. However, work commenced in the Autumn of 1940. The RAF Construction Branch (Work Service Section) and civilian contractors worked side by side building the base, and almost sixty years later some examples of their efforts still stand. Work began on the causeway from South Uist to Benbecula in 1938 but it took the outbreak of war to see it completed in 1941. By the last months of 1941, RAF servicing personnel began to arrive.

Stan Simmonds, now a resident on the island, remembers: 'I was told I was being posted to a place called BEN-BEE-COOLA. I thought this was great and asked if it was somewhere in the South Seas. I was told that it was an island "but certainly not in the South Seas".

'In late August 1941, I was one of a small group of airmen posted to RAF station Benbecula. We arrived at the RAF Embarkation Unit after a journey of twenty-six hours from Oban. We were given a sparse breakfast, issued with some blankets and taken to an empty Nissen hut. The hut had no furniture and it was some weeks before we were given beds. There was no electricity, the dining hall being illuminated by hurricane lamps. It was surprising how quickly the station built up, with new personnel arriving with every boat. Things slowly improved. Balivanich school was taken over for the officers' accommodation. Shortly

Operations room, RAF Benbecula. (Ayers)

Drinking beer from jam jars in the Lochboisdale Hotel. (Dyer)

A very rare bird: a B17 MK1 on convoy patrol. Mark 1 Flying Fortresses were briefly at Benbecula with 206 Squadron in 1942. (RAF Benbecula)

'Brasso and bike repairs'. Nissen hut life at RAF Benbecula. (Dyer)

after Christmas the second dining hall was opened up as a recreational area. It was in this hall also that we held the very first social event at RAF Benbecula. At this function I met an island girl who would later become my wife.'

In 1941 a WT/DF Signals section was located on the small island of Suneval, accessible at low tide off the north-west

corner of the airfield. 206 was the first operational Squadron to arrive, in 1942, with Hudsons and, later, B17 Flying Fortress. The Squadron achieved wonderful results against the U-boats and were joined by another Fortress Squadron, 220, in 1943. Between them twelve U-boat attacks were pressed home. Both squadrons left the island in October 1943.

When 206 Squadron arrived in Benbecula, they were still coming to terms with the fact that they had flown on the first 1000 Bomber raid to Germany a week before, during which their CO's plane and another crew were lost. Ted Nelson, one of those first 206 Squadron men, recalls: 'Going on leave from Benbec we drank beer out of a jam jar tied onto the bar with a string at the Lochboisdale Hotel, then endured the MacBraynes steamer to Oban.

'On 31 October we sighted and attacked with six DCs [depth charges] our first U-boat with an inconclusive result. On 11 June we set off on a search for Wing Commander Thompson and the crew of R/206, which had been shot down by a U-boat [this was one of the largest and most detailed searches of the war. The Fortress crew were eventually rescued by a Catalina]. We continued searching but were diverted to Iceland where we stocked up with all the unobtainables, including more chocolate than was probably available in the whole of Scotland! Returning to Benbecula we began to lose engine power. To lighten the aircraft we had to release our depth charges, then our guns and ammunition – everything stripped out to try to maintain height. Finally as we were getting closer and closer to the sea faster than we were getting to Benbecula, as a last resort the chocolate and all the other

Fortress crew get a last minute briefing before take-off at Benbecula. Australian Jack de la Rue was piloting his Fortress along the main runway in October 1942, about to take off, when another plane taxied across the runway. De la Rue's aircraft stalled and plunged into the sea with the loss of five crew. (Dyer)

American supplies went out the rear gun ports. We flew straight in at virtually zero feet, just making it.

'It was sad beyond words to go into the ops room and follow the progress of a convoy. First day, 120 ships, next visit 105 ships, next day 90, and so it went on, always fewer ships than the day before. They suffered so much.'

Professor Ian Donald, Medical Officer of 206 Squadron Benbecula. Professor Donald used the knowledge of sonar and radar he picked up in the RAF to good use when he pioneered ultra sound scans for pregnant women while Emeritus Professor of Midwifery at Rottenrow Hospital, Glasgow, in the 1950s. (Donald)

John Harrison, one of 206's ground crew, remembers: 'I was an ex-apprentice instrument maker and joined 206 Squadron in June 1941, serving with them on detachment in Stornoway in January to February 1942 and then in Benbecula. I remember the camaraderie which was strong in the squadron. It was nothing unusual for the air crew – after a gruelling four to five hour convoy patrol to remain with the ground crew, refuelling, rebombing, covering up and tying down the aircraft until one and two in the morning.'

Don Bryan was a Wireless Operator with 206. 'I vividly recall a tremendous gale that blew one night in December 1942. I was on orderly duty and I had no sleep the whole night. Hangar doors were blown down onto parked aircraft and there was quite a lot of damage. My crew were called in the morning to take off for a flight but I must have looked all in because I was told to stand down, someone else would take my place. The crew took off and never came back. My skipper had been Johnny Owen. On one patrol he attacked three seperate U-boats. He dropped DCs on the first two but only had machine gun bullets left to attack the third.'

A U-boat caught on the surface and under attack. (RAF Benbecula)

Squadron Leader Bob Cowey made the first of 206's successful U-boat sinkings on 27 October 1942 and a second on 24 April 1943. He was awarded a DFC. Of the second attack Cowey recalled: 'The U-boat gunners remained on deck and fired at us. This was a surprise and a new tactic. Our attack was pressed home and the U-boats rose up out of the water and sank leaving a number of men in the water. We could do little for them. Weather was reported as closing in at Benbecula and we had to divert to Iceland.'

Willis Roxburgh DFC wrote the following to a 206 colleague of his time at Benbecula: 'During the first week of January 1943 a special Naval Officer came to Benbecula. An expert on anti-U-boat warfare, this Naval Officer convened a meeting of captains of aircraft from the squadron. He told us some facts and described with graphs how we were just lapping over the maximum tonnage we could lose and still stay in the war. He reckoned that the U-boat war would be won or lost by May 1943 and we were authorised to abandon normal safety measures.'

Joe Griffith, a Canadian navigator with 206, was involved in a U-boat sinking with Roxburgh's crew in March 1943. 'We took off about 11.30 p.m. When we arrived at the search area it was still dark. Later as we came out of cloud the U-boat was sighted cutting across our path heading south-west fully surfaced and not more than two or three miles away. The accepted way to attack a U-boat was to get down to 50 feet altitude, level out, and attack diagonally across the length of the U-boat. There was no time to lose that height – the captain called for "bomb doors open" and he pushed the nose down and we became a dive bomber. We poured continuous machine gun fire into the conning tower of the U-boat – armour-piercing and tracer bullets. I have no idea what speed we reached in the dive. It was over in a matter of seconds. The two pilots were both busy pulling out of the dive. My position was in the nose of the

Willis Roxburgh DFC (centre) in front of a Flying Fortress at Benbecula with fellow pilots Wills and Peirse. Roxburgh turned the Fortress into a dive bomber to sink a U-boat on 25 March 1943.
(206 Sqn Assoc)

aircraft and I thought we were almost close enough to have touched the U-boat as we passed overhead.'

Richard Thomas was on that same flight. 'I can feel compassion for the forty-nine U-boat men who died on that bright day in March, but, at the time the only feeling among our young crew was one of wild elation. All the months of training, all the long hours spent flying over an unfriendly sea, all the searching by eye and radar had been brought to a fitting climax.

'As the official history of the war was to state, the fight to keep the sea-lanes open "was the most prolonged and complex battle in the history of naval warfare". My logbook records the length of the flight as being eleven hours ten minutes. I can remember nothing of the eleven hours out and back. Yet the ten minutes or so over the target are as vivid now as they were then.'

Peter Wooton worked in the Station Post Office at Benbecula in 1943. 'At the base we had Flying Officer Gate-Eastley [a stand-up comedian on post-war BBC radio], who offended the locals with a joke to the effect the island population was shrinking, because every time a new

An RAF man visits a traditional thatched croft on Benbecula. In the doorway stands the crofter and his son. Jim Romanes, the popular CO of 206 Squadron, remembers attending an RAF man's wedding reception in the girl's family croft byre and getting a gift of a bottle of 'Politician' whisky from the island priest. (Titchiner)

baby was born, around half-a-dozen young men left for the mainland. He was posted away after that although he re-peated it on the radio after the war.

'A number of cottages near the airfield were possible hazards to aircraft and so carried a red light on the roof. One of these was occupied by a lady of about sixty summers and her bed-ridden mother. She was an extremely sociable person and loved young people, be they island girls or RAF people. We would call in for a half hour or so in the evening

for a chat. When the Italian POWs arrived, they were without an interpreter for a while. Two of them seemed to have seen the red light and the comings and goings and come to a certain conclusion regarding the purpose of the establishment. One evening there was four of us round the peat fire – the householder, a most respectable local girl, the ENSA cinema operator and myself. Two Italians walked in, produced a sweater, pointed to the girl and said "half an hour". The other man and myself chased them out and

(Far left) An RAF man enjoying the peace and quiet of a trout loch on Benbecula. Note the peat stacks in the background. (Glebocki)

Very important members of the team: the NAAFI girls at RAF Benbecula. (McGillivray)

Highland games for locals and RAF at Benbecula, 1944. (Pringle)

then had the embarrassing task of explaining to the ladies what it was all about. However, it seems they decided that we only objected to the price and came back on several other days with more and more goods to barter until at last the services of the interpreter became available and the matter was cleared up.

'The camp cinema showed new films each week. Once we even held a "World Premiere". Some bodger in London sent us a copy of the film *Henry V* before it had been released and it arrived on the mail plane the day the official premiere was to be held in London. That evening we ran it three-quarters of an hour before it was seen by Royalty in Leicester Square.

'The NAAFI canteen, with its beer at reduced prices, was

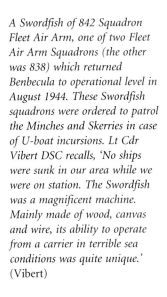

A Swordfish of 842 Squadron Fleet Air Arm, one of two Fleet Air Arm Squadrons (the other was 838) which returned Benbecula to operational level in August 1944. These Swordfish squadrons were ordered to patrol the Minches and Skerries in case of U-boat incursions. Lt Cdr Vibert DSC recalls, 'No ships were sunk in our area while we were on station. The Swordfish was a magnificent machine. Mainly made of wood, canvas and wire, its ability to operate from a carrier in terrible sea conditions was quite unique.' (Vibert)

officially open only to coast guards while they were on duty and not otherwise. The RAF never requested a copy of their duty roster. There would sometimes be as many as ten "coastguards" sitting in a line with glass in hand, disarming the duty corporal for the evening with a warm friendly greeting.

'Many of the families who made us so welcome to their homes had menfolk who were fighting the war in dangerous and uncomfortable conditions very different to those we enjoyed on Benbecula. In the very nature of service life, when we were moved from camp to camp, we rarely had

more than thirty-six hours notice to clear up our work and pack our kit, with no time to say "good-bye" and more importantly "thank you" to our friends.'

During 1944 304 (Polish) Squadron, who had been on Tiree in 1942, made a return to the Hebrides at Benbecula. The men of 304 had all fought at least one war to get out of occupied Poland, and some then fought in France only to start all over again with the RAF. This is an extract written by George Glebocki of 304 summing up the pain, fears and loneliness of young men fighting a war so far from home. 'Our quaint little isle, inhospitable and unfriendly as

FL/LT Leslek Miedzibrodski of 304 (Polish) Squadron with his crew and a Wellington which shows the signs of an 'argument' with a U-boat.

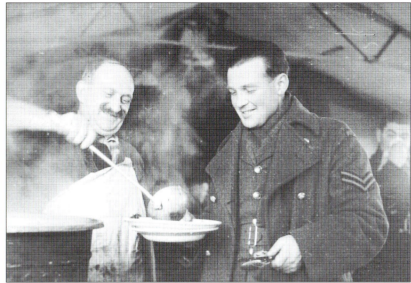

304 Polish Squadron's Mess, complete with their own cooks. When Bernard Poloniecki received a letter from Califonia from an ex–304 friend after the war, he read 'Missing Benbecula, rain and porridge'! (Watson)

Clearing the runway on Benbecula, January 1945. (Glebocki)

Andy McNab of 220 remembers, 'We had what was called Benbec stoop. This is caused by having to bend against the wind at an angle of forty-five degrees. It used to be said that when you got back onto the mainland you could tell someone who had been on Benbec by the way they walked.' (Glebocki)

Surrendered U-boat with RN boarding party, 11 May 1945. One of the final tasks of the war for 36 Squadron was to round up dozens of German U-boats. (Higgs)

it seemed at first, has many hidden charms. As if nature herself in recompense for bad weather and rain, wanted in the rare moments of respite, to stun and intoxicate us. Morning rose like many others, bathed in misty drizzle. A new flight was already hovering somewhere out over the icy Atlantic, tracking German U-boats, waging a cunning and ingenious war against the inventive skill of German engineers, and against the U-boat Schnorkel. An almost hopeless war. So many flights endured in vain in this terribly difficult struggle. So many hundreds of hours of torture, vomiting, engines and crews dying in wild, devilish burst of squalls, in the cruel clutch of icing 500 feet over the raging Atlantic. Till finally one morning in the grey dawn "X" for X-Ray, from our Squadron, reported that he was attacking a streak of smoke ahead of him. A flame growing from the water. He knew that it was the first and probably the last chance for attack. The explosion and a plume of foam blotted out the scene. When the water settled there was on the spot of the attack an ever-widening patch of shiny oil. That was all. Hundreds of flying hours for an attack lasting a few seconds.

'Night again lengthens and at last the wind falls. Slowly we leave the mess. This solitude on the island, this desertedness, this overlooking of all our work. The uncertainty of our fate and our morrow, and the wrong done against the living body of our nation, against all that is holy to us. What is the aim, the essence of this war? The wind catches our words and tosses them into space. We do not know whether it is the wind or the rain, or whether tears flow over our cheeks.' Written on Benbecula, Christmas 1944.

In November 1944 Harold Crossley was posted to RAF Benbecula. 'After being "chucked about" all day on the ferry and terribly sea-sick, we arrived at Loch Boisdale, South Uist, at 11 p.m. After two days medical attention for a strained stomach, I took up duties in the station photographic section. RAF Benbecula was made up of three areas: living site, messing site, technical site, each about a mile apart. The bike was a necessity but due to the wind that was always present you could only use it in the one direction. The crofts in those days were very primitive, usually with a pig lying in the door. The kitchen floor was earth with chickens pecking about. A local priest told me the story that Compton McKenzie wrote eight years later – *Whisky Galore*. He told us that two whisky dumps were made on Benbecula. One was lost when the RAF built a runway over it.'

Peter Hewlett recalls these times. 'At Benbecula I was a corporal employed in the Operations Room and Filter Room. It was there that plots on aircraft were received from Radar Stations, identified and passed to 15 Group Coastal Command Headquarters at Liverpool. One aircraft which we could always rely on whatever the weather was the Scottish Airways De Havilland Rapide. When it was just impossible to land the pilot flew as low as he could and dropped the newspaper and mail bag on to the airfield.

'Some fellows used to get sheep skins to make rugs. This seemed to be a favourite pastime for some of our Station Police. I doubt if the cells in the Guard Room were ever used for their intended purpose.'

36 Squadron was based at Benbecula from 9 March until its disbandment on 4 June 1945. Walter Higgs transferred to Benbecula in March 1945 with 36 Squadron. 'On VE day I went to a small Post Office somewhere near the aerodrome and handed a telegram form over to a stern looking lady. She read it, looked at me, then got on to a telephone. She burst into a language I had never heard before (or since), gesticulating, laughing as she explained to a person on the other end of the phone the contents of the cable to be sent to NZ. It said "Darling will you marry me?" It worked. My wife still has the cable in her top drawer.'

7
Tobermory

THE beauty of Tobermory Bay on the island of Mull is known worldwide, but the contribution made there to victory in World War Two deserves to be equally famed. Almost 1100 ships and crews 'worked up' at Tobermory; it was an intense period of training where mostly inexperienced men were welded into a ship's company ready to take on the U-boats. Over 130 U-boats were sunk by Tobermory trained crews and forty enemy aircraft confirmed shot down.

Although many thousands of sailors and civilians were linked to the Royal Navy base at Tobermory between 1940 and 1945, one legendary figure stands out as being responsible for the achievements of the base. That man was Vice Admiral Sir Gilbert Stephenson. Although over 60 years of age, Stephenson came out of retirement in 1939 on the day war began. He had served in the Royal Navy in World War One, and indeed for some time before that, and had commanded the Portsmouth barracks in the 1920s. On resuming service in World War Two he was Commodore in early convoys crossing the North Atlantic and was also involved in the withdrawal at Dunkirk as one of the beach masters. He was given the task of setting up and running an anti-U-boat working up base, and Tobermory was chosen. Stephenson, sometimes known as 'Monkey', perhaps because of his agility and his large grey whiskers, was admired, dreaded and held in great respect by the crews who visited Tobermory. It is of real testimony to Stephenson that many of the procedures and practices he developed at Tobermory continued to form the basis of Royal Navy training at Portland for many decades after World War Two. He was deservedly knighted in 1943.

Stephenson chose experienced crew to set up his base, HMS *Western Isles*. Most of them had World War One service or were survivors from the Narvik campaign or Atlantic convoys. Among Stephenson's staff in 1943 was John Grant (later Rear Admiral) who rewrote Admiralty manuals on anti-U-Boat warfare and was regarded as one of the chief architects of victory in the Atlantic.

Tobermory Bay in wartime.
(Hague)

Nancy Stephenson, the daughter of Vice Admiral Stephenson, remembers these times. 'I shall never forget my first visit to Scotland. My mother and I arrived at Oban in the middle of the war to visit my father. I was greeted by the beautiful sight of the bay full of ships such as corvettes and sloops. Visiting *Western Isles* was a real treat for me. All my life I had loved ships. Whenever mother was staying at Tobermory she would spend the day in my father's cabin sewing and reading. Being with him was all she wanted. She would come ashore in the evening to the Western Isles Hotel, though he himself never slept ashore. I remember one cold stormy night an SOS call came from a corvette in difficulty trying to get in to the bay with a new captain and crew. My father immediately set of in his barge and brought it in himself.

'The Allan family of Aros took us under their wing. They had a big house and three little girls. I'm sure the girls saved my father's sanity. They treated him as an equal whereas the rest of the community were always in awe of him. I do think the awe was mixed with deep affection though. My father was a keen gardner and had an allotment on Calve Island on which his chief crop was spinach. He grew this especially for the children of his staff. Mrs McKenzie, the Minister's wife, acted as his main liaison with Tobermory people.'

Peter Dawson and Bob Cave were on that first *Western Isles* (the former Isle of Man ferry, *Tynewald*). They remember leaving Glasgow just after an air raid and arriving at Tobermory followed by HMS *Alecto*, a submarine depot ship, with two subs for training. Lectures soon began on

HMS Western Isles *officers with Sir Gilbert Stephenson (centre row, fifth from right).* (Grumbridge)

(Left) HMS Western Isles *crew coming ashore. George McCaldon recalls, 'I was often ashore in the evenings as a watch keeper. I just don't know how we got a Liberty boat full of sailors back to their ships in the bay in total darkness!'* (Mull Museum)

A frigate towing targets for gunnery practice. The yacht Shaharazad *is in the background.* (Reid)

(Right) A crowded scene in Tobermory Bay in wartime, including a captured U-boat (far right). This would have been a secretly taken photograph. (Ellis)

Asdic, radar, ship recognition and so on. A waterfall into the bay was turned into fresh water supply for ships by creating a chute with sail canvas.

Jack Crummey was Leading Telegraphist on HMS *Western Isles*. 'We sailed into Tobermory in July 1940 on a dark, misty, rainy Sunday morning. The main street was deserted – no doubt the church was full. At Tobermory ninety to ninety-five percent of all naval personnel undergoing training were HOs (hostilities only) and serving in their first ship. Their real training would of course be later on in North Atlantic and Acrtic convoys. The Minches and the Sound of Mull were our "playgrounds". At Tobermory we had a Norweigan submarine, the B1, which was used continuously for mock attacks by ships undergoing training. She was attacked with small canisters with detonators used as depth charges. To get respite on board we used to settle gently on a sandy shelf near the Dutchman's Cap Island and lie "doggo" and have a brew in piece and quiet. Then back on with the war.

'Social life at Tobermory was at a premium. Most of the local girls had been studied and voted upon by the visual communication staff of *Western Isles*. On the bridge was a powerful telescope.'

Jim Garsides was at Tobermory twice on new escort vessels. 'On one occasion our First Leuitenant was called

The second HMS Western Isles *in Tobermory Bay. Solitary figure on rear deck may be the 'Terror' (Stephenson) himself.* (Ellis)

aboard HMS *Western Isles*, and we never saw him again. On another occasion after a march past on Tobermory front Stephenson gave the officers a dressing down. It must have worked well. On our first convoy to Freetown West Africa we caught U–123 on the surface. There were no survivors'.

Cyril Grumbridge was an officer on the team of HMS *Western Isles* from 1942 until the end of hostilities. The officers were involved in training but had to be available for immediate transfer to a working up vessel should circumstances prove necessary. 'My wife lost our child in the blitz in London. The Brown family of Tobermory kindly invited her to live with them to help her recuperate. Stephenson was a very religious man, but his object was to win the war therefore training had to be done on Sundays. He must have offended the RC hierarchy as they sent a priest to reminstrate with him. After forty-five minutes in the Commodore's cabin I interrupted the interview as

A wartime wedding in Tobermory. (Ellis)

(Far right) Wrens waiting to go on leave from Tobermory pier. Helen Biggin (second left) was a Wren Torpedowoman working at the distillery. Just before VJ Day she got an afternoon off to go on a picnic. As she looked down on the bay she heard an explosion. Her replacement for the day working with detonators, was killed, and a number of others were injured. It was a sad end to the war at Tobermory. (Biggin)

Officer of the Watch, with others wishing to see the chaplain. I apologised to the Commodore later. However, he replied "That's alright 'Grum', had you given me another ten minutes I would have converted him!'"

Dr David llingworth recalls his time at Tobermory. 'In April 1944 I was surgeon on HMS *Lochkillin*. She was crammed with remarkably sophisticated devices for locating and destroying U-boats. We entered the Bay between several war ships with HMS *Western Isles*, an ancient looking vessel tied up to the pier. This floating Naval

Headquarters looked gloomy and sinister but the town was enchanting.

'Admiral Sir Gilbert Stephenson was small, wrinkled and with great tufts of hair sprouting from his malar bones. I thought at once that I was looking at a war time phenomenon – a creature generated at just the right time to fulfil a portentous purpose, like Churchill or Montgomery. He emanated a chilling tension. I was convinced that I would get an electric shock if I touched him. He was obsessional and meticulous and totally dedicated. As a result most of those who took a ship into Tobermory found the enemy much less troublesome than "Monkey". Stephenson once ordered me to get a sailor (our cook) down from the crows' nest in a stretcher pretending he was a casualty. The captain told me later that he had hoped we would drop him as the food he served up was not really edible.

'"Angle of sight first and then describe what you see" was Monkey's oft-repeated slogan. This was to save the *'killin* when two torpedoes homed in on us some weeks later. But we hit the U-boat and avoided the torpedoes a fraction of a second before certain death overcame us. And now it is too late to say "thank you".

'Each evening we returned to Tobermory, exhausted in mind but eager to take the liberty boat to the pier and the relaxation of the Western Isles Hotel. The balance between victory and defeat is so delicate that Tobermory may well have been the critical factor.'

Janet Bownrigg was a leading Wren and Petty Officer cook at HMS *Western Isles*. 'I would do the baking for the Commodore's cocktail parties. My records for Tobermory show an above average for efficiency. The Commodore must have enjoyed the baking. On reporting to the Commodore to request leave he would often say "Not granted". When we had to go on board *Western Isles* for discussion groups we were ordered to wear "blackout knickers" for climbing the ladders. We Wrens lived in two large houses, Oakwood and Dunard. Our main entertainment was going

(Far left) A swimming gala held from the gunnery targets as part of the VE Celebrations in Tobermory. (Ellis)

RN men and Wrens who worked at Tobermory Distillery. Edgar Holden was at Tobermory from August to December 1941. 'When I was on guard duty at the distillery building, we were guarding three or four hundred depth charges. One false move and the whole island would have been gone for ever.' (Ellis)

down to see who and what came off the *Lochinvar* ferry each afternoon'.

Lieutenant Commander Douglas Orr RVNR remembers: 'In 1941 I was in command of HMS *Greenfly*, an anti-sub-marine/mine-sweeping trawler. Arriving at Tobermory our entire ships' company of some 45 men were summoned and addressed by Vice Admiral Stephenson himself. He did this with an intensity that could not be matched by many men. Thinking of the "Terror of Tobermory" I am always reminded of his passion for efficiency – to win the war. "That's why you are here" he would say. We were at Tobermory over the Christmas period. In fact we were sent to Oban on Christmas day itself to coal the ship.'

Tony Goldsmith served on HMS *Western Isles* from July to September 1945 as an RNVR Sub Lt. Although the German War was over, escort vessels were still being worked up at Tobermory. Vice Admiral Stephenson had not eased up at all. 'I saw one frigate arrive and make rather a hash of securing to a buoy. Unfortunately the Admiral saw this and ordered the frigate to sail out and return to Tobermory again and again, throughout the day, until he was satisfied. I was accommodated in the yacht *The Lady Blanche* moored alongside the *Western Isles*. On one occasion I was invited to lunch with the Admiral and found him such a kindly old gentleman. He ceased to be so on spying, through his tele-scope, a drunken sailor emerge from The MacDonald Arms. He promptly put the establishment out of bounds.'

Dr David Ilingworth has a final thought on this wartime base. 'Tobermory tipped the balance just enough, I believe, for us to beat the U-boats before the enemy choked us into submission. It was a closer run thing than Waterloo and Tobermory has not received the credit it deserves.'

8

Women in the Services

DESPITE answering the call with distinction in the First World War, all three women's services (Army, Navy and Air Force) were disbanded. Astonishing as it may now seem, recruitment of women in numbers to the services was almost left calamitously late. The Auxiliary Territorial Service (ATS) was formed in September 1938. The Women's Royal Naval Service (WRNS or Wrens) was reformed in March 1939. The Womens Auxiliary Air Force (WAAFs) did not come into being until June 1939. For the first two and a half years of the war all women who served were volunteers, then the government passed the National Service Act (No. 2) in December 1941 which ushered in conscription of women.

Women also contributed to the war effort in countless other roles, to say nothing of their influence on morale, spirit and fortitude. They played their part through the Land Army, The Women's Forestry Service, nursing services, Air Raid Precautions (ARP), the Navy Army and

WAAFs v Wrens at soccer, Mossfield Park Oban 1944. (Baillie)

WAAFs relax outside Burnbank (WAAF quarters and RAF medical centre). (Williams)

(Far right) WAAFs in 'Mae Wests' at Dungallan, before a flight in a Sunderland organised to help the wireless operators get a better understanding about what conditions were like on an operational flight. (Williams)

ghost boy at Dungallan ever hears, in some dimension beyond our hearing, that wonderful, never forgotten roar, and turns to watch a phantom Sunderland flying off into silent dawn of a long-gone yesterday.'

Dorothy Williams also worked at Dungallan. 'We worked a three watch system, seven days a week, 365 days a year. Sleeping was not easy. Once the MO insisted the WAAF wireless operators had a week in hospital to sleep.

'The Signals Officer decided we would have a better understanding of the atmospheric and other problems of aircrew wireless operators if we experienced it first hand. We had a couple of local flights until a shocking landing was made. The station CO witnessed this. No more WAAF flying.'

Wendy Austin Bishop was a WAAF nurse. 'I was eighteen years of age and it was my first visit to Scotland. I remember the journey well, by steam train crowded with service personnel, with the bewitching beauty of the hills and mountains and the uncanny feeling of going into cloud as the train sped north.

'I hauled my kit bag out of the station and heard the gulls shrieking, saw the fishing boats and the Folly monument towering above the town, the colour of all the uniforms, the hustle and bustle. Across the bay Catalina and Sunderland aircraft bobbed on the waves with the sun shining on their wings. That, to me, was Oban in wartime.'

Esther(Grant) Baillie was a WAAF driver at Oban for almost three years from 1942. She once drove across the Connel bridge thirty-two times in one day, helping set up the RAF camp at North Connel. 'On one occasion American servicemen arrived in Oban from one of the islands where they had been on survival exercises for some time. They were billeted in the Columba Hotel on the North Pier, and suddenly realised that the building across the road [the Argyll Hotel] was full of WAAFs. Next thing, they were trying to get up the drainpipes at the back of the Argyll, so the SPs had to be called out to get them down.'

Daphne Dagg remembers: 'I was billeted in the Alexandra Hotel, supplied with a bicycle, told my hours of duty and then left to find my way to Dungallan House where the code and cypher rooms were. Late at night, after my first duty, I cycled back to the hotel – very cold and wet – and asked the barman for a drink. He refused to give me one, saying "you're not a guest – you're a billet".'

Kathleen (Wilson) Brakes was posted to Oban in January 1944 as a mechanic to work on Sunderland and Catalina flying boats. 'I can honestly say this was one of the happiest times of my life. We worked at Ganavan Sands in all weathers. I remember the Firth of Lorne being full with American ships gathering for D-Day in 1944. We were invited out to one for dinner and a tour of the ships. We were amazed at the lavish dinner provided.

'I did once have a pleasant flight over the Hebrides in a Catalina and at the same time the crew played a trick on me. The crew was South African and they were known for being mischievous. When we were airborne the co-pilot suggested I move into his seat as the views were wonderful. After five or ten minutes the pilot said he would like to see the navigator and wouldn't be long. He explained how to

WAAFs and RAF men inside the YWCA canteen at Corran Green, Oban. (Saunders)

fix a line on the horizon and if I kept it straight we would be OK. He disappeared into the back of the fuselage and I was alone – panic stricken. When the two pilots returned they casually explained I need not have worried as we were on automatic pilot.'

Ruby Brown was stationed at Oban and worked in the battery store on Kerrera. 'I went on flare path duty in small boats when flying boats were taking off and landing. Once a Catalina hit the shore on the Oban side while landing. We managed to get the crew out. On another occasion we had to land the bodies of Canadian airmen at Oban pier after a Sunderland crashed.

'I used to sing at RAF concert parties in the Great Western Hotel with Buddy Logan. On VE night at Oban there

RAF transport personnel behind Great Western Garage, Dunollie Road, Oban. (Baillie)

was a firework display on Kerrera. We had a drink and sing song in the Argyll then out in the street with dancing and music.'

Wrens

Wrens were stationed at Oban and later at Tobermory during the war from 1940 onwards. One of the first Wrens at Oban in May 1940 was Third Officer Jean C Smith. 'At first there was only about a dozen Wrens living in their own home [classed as "Immobile" Wrens]. Then some young girls from the south arrived, often very homesick. Work on war news in code and cypher, began to increase rapidly in 1940.'

Dorothy Pepper was a VS (Visual Signals) Wren. 'We worked on Oban railway pier, in our bell bottom trousers,

visited Oban stayed at the Alexandra Hotel. We signalled sweet nothings to each other across the bay by torch.'

Nan (Dunn) McKenzie worked in signals at RN HQ Oban from April 1943 to November 1944. 'We sent and received messages on the scrambler and took reams of shipping movements from the teleprinter to the cypher officer. We often had invitations to attend dances given by the RAF. On one occasion an officer ordered a WRN petty officer to accompany us as a chaperon. She sat and read a book all night.'

Joan Roberts did duty at the pier signal station. One dark night she and her colleague got strange tasting sandwiches. They threw them to the gulls. Next morning they were told they had been given chicken (the first time for years!). Flora McKechnie was a Wren at Oban in 1945. 'On 7 May I was awakened by the sound of laughter and cheering. A crowd of girls burst into my room saying the war had ended. A

Princess Marina, Duchess of Kent, at the Station Hotel in Oban (using the tradesmen and ratings entrance) in 1941. The Duchess was Commodore of Wrens. (Draper)

(Far left) Wrens in front of the gatehouse to Dunollie Estate, Oban. (McLundie)

which were most comfortable. Our signal station was by the railway sidings with empty goods wagons and carriages on either side. We had a small tower and cabin. On the platform was a fixed Aldis lamp and mast for flag signalling. We Wrens worked in pairs. Usually with me was my friend Rosemary Salt. Officers who telephoned and asked who was on duty often thought we were playing practical jokes. My husband was a Signals Officer in the Navy and when he

Margaret Kane (left) and Violet McGilivray (right) of the Women's Forestry Service, Barcaldine. (Valbonesi)

Women's Forestry Service at Barcaldine in working clothes. (Valbonesi)

gala day materialised without preparation. The old ferry *Lochinvar* came into the Bay, her flags flying and a piper playing on the deck. We did the Palais Glide and Lambeth Walk in a line across George Street holding up traffic. The merry making went on throughout the day and night. We were allowed out until 23.59 p.m. that night, which was very special.'

Violet McGillivray was at the Home Farm on Barcaldine Estate with the Womens Forestry Service from 1941 to 1945. Other camps in the area included Glen Etive, Bridge of Orchy, Lochaline, Morvern and Ardrishaig. 'Having worked in an office in Glasgow this was a very different lifestyle. To get to Oban for cinema or dances the girls had to cycle and if they returned after 11.00 p.m. Connel Bridge was "closed" and bikes had to be lifted over the gate.'

Margaret (Kane) Valbanesi was offered the Women's Forestry Service in 1944 as WAAFs and Wrens were not needed. At Barcaldine she worked from 8.00 a.m. to 5.00 p.m. with Saturday afternoon and Sunday off. 'It was back breaking using cross-cut saws. Our uniform was khaki jumper, breeches, oilskin coat with dungarees or overalls. My pay was 47 shillings a week.'

9

Islay, Stornoway and Other Bases

THE years 1940 to 1943 saw the RAF establish a presence on a number of Hebridean islands in the form of full airfields and various radio, radar and observation units. In late 1940 998 Port Operating Company of the Royal Engineers arrived at Oban to begin co-ordinating construction work. They worked at Tiree, Benbecula and Stornoway (as well as Aultbea), supposedly on the direct orders of Churchill to build airstrips that would deliver greater air coverage of the Atlantic. Following 998, 5007 (Construction) Squadron RAF were next on the scene, working with civilian contractors at Islay, Tiree and Benbecula airfields. They also built WT/DF stations on Kerrera and Colonsay along with

Wings for Victory day being celebrated by RAF visitors and barefoot pupils outside Lochboisdale school, 1943. (Fitzgibbons)

RAF Air Sea Rescue high speed launch in action. This was based at Port Ellen, Islay. (Overend)

Bowmore as seen from a flying boat looking down on Loch Indaal where two Sunderlands are moored. The famous round church in the foreground. (Museum of Islay Life)

a W/T post at Pennyfuir, Oban, and improved the facilities at Connel airfield. The A85 road leading to Oban was practically rebuilt for long vehicles carrying vital materials which were then transferred out to the various outlying bases.

RAF Islay

The RAF had a presence on Islay in a variety of guises from 1940 onwards. The airfield at Glenegadale was first used by Anson aircraft of 48 Squadron in 1941. Beaufighters of 304 Ferry Training Unit were based here during 1943, and indeed throughout the war Glenegadale played an important role as an emergency landing site and diversions were regular from Macrihanish and other Hebridean bases. The airfield featured briefly in the Crown Film Unit's wonderful film *Coastal Command*, which also had some great footage of the flying boat base at Bowmore. (By the time the film was released in Autumn 1942, the majority of the Sunderland crew depicted in the film had died in action, some going down in the plane which was carrying the Duke of

Crew of ASR launch and maintenance personnel at Port Ellen in the summer of 1943. (Overend)

Kent.) Port Ellen was the first admin site for Glenegaldale and was also a base for Air Sea Rescue launches.

Idris Jones was with the RAF on Islay from August 1940 until April 1942. 'I was one of the first five airmen to land on the island to open up RAF Port Ellen. Our headquarters were in Port Ellen distillery, and we were fortunate to be billeted in private houses near by. We oversaw the building of the airfield and the establishment of the flying boat station at Bowmore. When 48 Squadron were posted to Northern Ireland, many men and equipment went by RAF pinnaces. Disaster almost struck when one overturned, but the ferry *Lochiel* diverted to rescue them.'

The base at Bowmore was, over a lengthy period, an alternative site to Oban as an operational and training base for flying boats. Before World War Two, Short Brothers of Kent built flying boats for Imperial Airways known as 'G'

boats. When war broke out these G boats were put into use by the RAF and were converted to have three gun turrets – two amidships and one in the tail. A special unit was formed named G Flight, which was sent to Bowmore due to the large expanses of water on Loch Indaal. Bowmore flying boat base was officially established in December 1940. In March 1941 G flight was redesignated 119 Squadron and at the same time two more ex-Imperial Airways flying boats arrived at the unit. These were C class boats 'Clio' and 'Cordelia'. The G boats left Bowmore in July 1941. On 22 August 1941 Clio crashed at Bruichladdich, the reason being given as engine failure. 119 Squadron moved to Pembroke Dock, Wales, in August 1941.

246 Squadron, flying Sunderlands, formed here in late 1942 and remained briefly, until April 1943. A 246 Sunderland crashed in dramatic and tragic circumstances on 24

A Sunderland moored on a choppy Loch Indaal. Norman Geal of 246 Squadron can remember his skipper at a Sunderland controls continuously for almost two days helping avoid the 'Kite' being blown ashore during one of the livelier storms which would roll off the Atlantic. On one occasion during high winds and a hail storm, Geal and his crewmates had to lie on the wings to help hold down the Sunderland. (Museum of Islay Life)

(Far right) RAF men and WAAFs from RAF Saligo Bay relax on the beach while off duty. (Gribble)

'C' Class Imperial Airways flying boat in RAF service at Loch Indaal. (Thomas)

The Mess Hall at RAF Saligo Bay (Chain Home Low) radar station decorated for the Christmas dance, 1942. The floor is chalked for dancing. On Islay in wartime, dances were regularly held and could include big band waltzes, bagpiping and Gaelic singing. (Gribble)

January 1943. Coming into land near Blackrock at the head of Loch Indaal it clipped a cottage roof, bounced on the road (leaving metal embedded for many years) and crashed on the edge of the loch. The crew, though most were injured, got free, only to discover the rear gunner was still trapped on board. They returned to the stricken Sunderland but the depth charges exploded at this point killing nine of the twelve crew members.

During the summer of that year detachments of 422 Squadron RCAF (Royal Canadian Air Force) flew Sunderlands from the base. Crews would test depth charges by dropping one while returning to base. Local fishermen would be notified to bring in the stunned fish! Groups of children would also gather at Bowmore pier as each Sunderland crew returned and often they were rewarded with chewing gum and chocolate. On 25 May 1943 one of 422's Sunderlands crashed into the sea off Clare Isle on the west coast of Ireland while returning from convoy escort, with the loss of all crew.

Over the course of the war, a great deal of ground around Bowmore was taken over and built on by the RAF, with the distillery becoming flying HQ with an ops room and workshop. The Round Church and Loch Indaal are shown to great effect in action shots in the film *Coastal Command*.

The last RAF planes to use Islay were Mosquitoes from the (MAAE) Marine Aircraft Experimental Station which carried out trials on 'Highball', a version of the bouncing bomb. Sadly one plane with its two crewmen was lost in low flying in Saligo Bay in 1945.

RAF Unit Ardnamurchan

Pat Shute was posted to number 18 Wireless Observer Unit and sent to Ardnamurchan Point in 1941. 'Here we occupied two Nissen huts which served as sleeping quarters, mess, cook house and stores. They were situated overlooking a small bay below the point. The observer post and wireless shack were on the head land above the lighthouse. Our job was to watch the skies for aircraft, identify them, plot height and course and transmit details to Oban.

'At the nearby village of Portuairk we were made most welcome. We were allowed one liberty run in our truck per week. We saved this for Sunday and picked up local folk on the road going to the Kirk at Kilchoan. It was our way of repaying their kindness.'

RAF Colonsay

As a forward navigational aid site for RAF Oban, Colonsay was home to a radar beacon, a flashing beacon with morse

Members of the RAF unit at Kiloran, Colonsay, 1942. (Brown)

The MacBraynes steamer Hebrides at Coll. A rowing boat would bring out people, sheep and cattle. (McKinnon)

Inside a Nissen hut at RAF Carsaig, Mull. (Baldwin)

signal and HF/DF signals. Supplies came from Oban by RAF pinnace once a week, weather permitting.

There were two units, one at Kiloran and the other at Machrins. The RAF had to generate their own electricity at these camps. No vehicles had been permitted on the island by the laird pre-war, and it is possible that the only RAF horse and cart drivers in World War Two served here!

RAF Coll

In 1942 Peter Whitworth found himself posted to a network of wireless units whose local HQ was on Albany Street, Oban. 'We had units on Iona, Mull, Ardnamurchan, Colonsay and Tiree and Coll. Our unit on Coll was located about two miles from Arinagour in a pre-war shooting lodge, from where we plotted aircraft twenty-four hours a day. We were the only military on the island and so had to deal with any bodies washed ashore. We would occasionally plot unidentified or German aircraft and sometimes see Allied aircraft coming back with engines out or having suffered damage in action.'

RAF Carsaig (Mull)

Freddie Baldwin, an RAF radar operator, remembers: 'I was stationed at Carsaig from November 1941 to June 1942. There were about fifty RAF men there altogether. Carsaig was a Chain Home Low radar station. We were regularly in contact with the RAF at Tiree where we would send our plots of aircraft and boats. We occasionally visited Pennygael and the village hall at Bunessan where we played badminton by oil light.'

Lochboisdale

Ron Wickens was posted to 35 EU (Embarkation Unit) at Balivanich, Benbecula, in December 1941. 'After most of our building work was completed the unit moved to Lochboisdale, South Uist, and remained there until 1945. Our camp site at Lochboisdale is now a housing estate. Our unit consisted of about fifty RAF drivers and mechanics, along with thirty GD [General duties] men such as cooks, telephone operators, medical orderlies, store keepers and others. Our main duties concerned transporting everything that came ashore for RAF Benbecula. There was a small NAAFI run by a manageress and local girls, and ENSA shows and films would be put on from time to time, along with occasional dances. A very good relationship existed between the islanders and us "erks".'

No 62 Air Sea Rescue Unit were also based at Lochboisdale and had medical facilities on the launches and at their base which was situated behind the Lochboisdale hotel.

Bus to Benbecula at Lochboisdale, 1942. (Wickens)

An Avro Anson of 48 Squadron. Ansons were the first aircraft to fly operational sorties from the Hebrides during the war. In 1940, 612 County of Aberdeen Squadron were flying them from Stornoway golf course! In 1941, 48 Squadron flew Ansons out of Islay and Stornoway on convoy protection anti-U-boat patrols. The Anson served the RAF for over 30 years. (Dews)

The SS Politician *of the Harrison Line ran aground on rocks between the north of the Island of Eriskay and South Uist on 5 February 1941. She was carrying a mixed cargo of RAF stores, currency and the now legendary 22,000 cases of whisky. She was bound for the West Indies and to this day great controversy surrounds the exact nature of the contents of her holds when she foundered in those stormy Hebrid- ean waters. Sir Compton Mac- Kenzie produced a hilarious book* Whisky Galore *and there followed a superb film directed by Alexander McKendrick. Mysteriously, certain goverment papers relating to this sinking are subject to a non-disclosure ruling for 75 years. (Harrison Line)*

A Handley Page Harrow of 271 Squadron. This squadron flew these amazing large transport aircraft to the Hebrides and other Scottish islands in 1941 and 1942 on the 'Cabbage Run' delivering vital fresh vegetables. (Hartley)

RAF Barra

Bob Walker was one of the first RAF men posted to the island in 1941. He recalls one occasion when five Norweigan seamen came ashore in a dinghy. 'Invasion fears were very strong and they were immediately whisked off to Oban believed to be spies.'

Neville Knox spent some time at this split location unit. 'In December 1941 as a corporal in the RAF, I was posted to Barra, Grien Head CHL [Chain Home Low] station. Our work involved tracking both friendly and enemy aircraft. Ours could be identified by IFF [Identify Friend or Foe] intermittent blips on the screen. While there I broke my leg playing football, and as we had no Medical Officer I had to travel nearly 200 miles by land and sea on my own to a Glasgow hospital to have it set.'

RAF men beachcombing on Barra, 1942. (Rowland)

Arthur Rowland was based at Tangusdale RAF camp, Barra, which was some six miles from the radar post at Grien Head. 'One of our Nissen huts served as a NAAFI. We had a piano and wind-up gramophone but only two records. Occasionally the locals had a ceilidh which began with a whist drive. The floor was cleared and brushed, then someone would pump up the acetyline lamps and the eightsome reels began. Castlebay had one pub, but in those days no women were allowed in!'

Freddie Jenkins was part of the RAF Communications Flight at Abbotsinch airport, Glasgow. They covered all the Scottish islands with airfields (and many with only beaches). 'Sollas, North Uist was a favourite because of hospitality at the Lochmaddy Hotel. We mostly flew De Havilland Rapides but also made use of an old Dutch Fokker 22 aircraft. This large, four-engined plane even landed on the beach at Barra on occasion (to pick up some of the cargo from the SS *Politician*) but came to grief carrying RAF men home on leave from the Hebrides when it crashed into West Loch Tarbert in July 1943.'

RAF Stornoway

Although the northerly situation of Stornoway meant that it was ideally suited for observer and radar purposes, the RAF's plans for a base were complicated by a disagreement over whether or not Stornoway golf course should become an airstrip. Decisive action was taken by the RAF and the first operational squadron was a detachment from 612 in 1940 (Ansons) and 48 Squadron, which arrived in July 1941 with Anson aircraft and later Hudsons. The Officers' Mess was at Lewis Castle and was shared with Royal Navy officers. 701 Fleet Air Arm Squadron flew Walrus flying boats from Stornoway during 1940 and 1941. Other FAA squadrons made use of the airfield between 1941 and 1944. During the summer of 1942 500 Squadron (Hudsons) flew from

A De Havilland Dominie of the RAF Communications Flight based at Abbotsinch near Glasgow coming into Tiree from the north west. These aircraft were an important link to many of the Hebridean Islands during wartime. (Brock)

SOUTH BEACH, STORNOWAY.

Stornoway as it would have looked early in World War Two. (McCusker)

Stornoway, making a number of U-boat attacks and engaging in combat with long range Luftwaffe aircraft.

Over the course of the war, the airfield at Stornoway played a vital role as a staging post used by vast numbers of US aircraft coming across to the UK via Iceland. The US airmen stopping off there would often leave clothing and underwear in the billets when they left, which were very valuable to British men suffering wartime clothing rationing.

Other postings to Stornoway during the war were 66 Air Sea Rescue Unit, which operated launches from the harbour, 58 Squadron, who came first in 1942 flying Whitley bombers, 303 FTU, which trained Wellington crews at Stornoway during 1943 and early 1944, and 518 Met Squadron, who were briefly at Stornoway in 1943. From August 1944 to the end of World War Two Stornoway was home to 58 and 502 squadrons (Coastal Command) flying Halifax aircraft. These two squadrons flew anti-shipping strikes in the Kattegat and Skagerrak seas and delivered outstanding results in their attacks and harassed and sank German shipping to the very end of the European war.

During World War Two There were a number of aircraft crashes on or around Stornoway airfield with losses of life. A Hudson of 500 Squadron crashed on 31 July 1942 killing

all crew. On 19 September 1942 a Whitley of 58 Squadron landed on the outskirts of Stornoway with a load of depth charges still on board. The crew of five were all badly burned and eventually treated by the famous plastic surgeon Sir Archibald McIndoe. A (US) B36 Marauder aircraft crashed off the runway on 24 June 1944 killing two airmen and seriously injuring the other crew. Halifax HR792 of 58 Squadron made a belly landing on 13 January 1945 and was scrapped. Part of the fuselage spent more than forty years as a hen house on the island before being recovered to form part of a restored Halifax at Elvington, Yorkshire.

1944 and 1945 saw the Allies really begin to hit back, with Stornoway playing an important part in the offensive. Squadron Leader Hardwick Holderness DSO DFC AFC (CO of 502 Squadron), a Rhodesian in the RAF, believes: 'The contribution made by 502 and 58 Squadrons at Stornoway during the winter and spring of 1944/45 towards bringing to a successful end the war against Nazi Germany was something quite exceptional. Our anti-shipping technique in the

502 Squadron line up with a Halifax, Stornoway 1945. (McLaren)

Briefing at RAF Stornoway. (Swain)

Skagerrak and Kattegat seas involved extraordinary team work and dedication. Our on-board radar equipment was primitive by today's standards – the navigator used dead reckoning and the pilot had to cross the north coast of

A Halifax crew of 502 Squadron before an 'op'. (McLaren)

Scotland then the North Sea often in atrocious weather conditions, to say nothing of making bombing runs and evading night fighters. All the while the WOP/AGs were on constant lookout. Backing this up ground crews worked in the full force of North Atlantic weather maintaining aircraft to an extremely high standard.'

John Davenport DFC has strong memories of flying as a pilot with 502 Squadron at Stornoway. 'We took off from Stornoway on 25 January 1945 with orders to patrol between Aalesund and Kristiansund. After about four hours we picked up two contacts on the radar miles ahead. We dropped flame floats, and then made an approach towards the ships in the moonpath on the water. We made three hits. We dropped to fifty feet and made away at full speed. On the night of 21/22 April 1945 we took off fully loaded with seven 500-pound bombs, flares, flame floats, photo flash etc. and fuel for twelve hours. At 0115 hours we sighted three large ships in Fredrikhaven harbour and turned towards them for attack with flak from the ships and land. We made at least two, possibly three, direct hits on a large ship. There was a huge orange explosion and

white smoke. I received the DFC for these attacks and my expert navigator John O'Kane the DFM. It wasn't until almost fifty years later in correspondence with Air Historical Branch that I was able to confirm we sunk the German ship *Pergamon* (with no casualties!) on 25 January 1945 and the *Neukuhren* on 21 April.

'One chap on the other squadron at Stornoway at the time had an incredible escape. During a night attack in the Kattegat, their Halifax received a direct hit. When the crew checked an enormous hole had been blown underneath, and there was no sign of one wireless operator. On the

(Far left) John Davenport DFC at the controls of a Coastal Command Halifax, Stornoway. (Davenport)

Sinking German cargo vessel Neukuhren. (Davenport)

Halifax showing the damaged area where a crew member hung underneath by his parachute 'D' ring for over two hours. (Davenport)

'V for Victory'. Ready to go, but the war is over, May 1945. (Swain)

return journey to Stornoway they were redirected to Carnaby in Yorkshire, an emergency landing field. After over two hours flying they arrived. When they got down they discovered to their great surprise and delight that the wireless operator was hanging precariously underneath the Halifax, suspended merely by a "D" ring on his parachute harness caught on some jagged metal. He was semi-conscious and extremely cold but remarkably still alive.'

Edith (McCoy) Burke was the Signals Officers' clerk in the operations block at Stornoway. 'The Duty Officer often got me to accompany him to outstations at Barvas and Dell at the Butt of Lewis. As we travelled we saw ladies weaving tweed which they had already dyed and spun. Miles from anywhere we would pass old ladies with massive loads on their backs – I think it was peat. Although we offered a lift many times, they would never accept.'

Deryck McCusker also flew from Stornoway with 58 Squadron during 1944/45. 'Iron ore was vital for the enemy's industry and much of this was supplied from Scandinavia. It was shipped by sea from the Narvik mining sites. Our attacks were really an entrepreneurial form of exercise very much left to individual skippers and crews to assess the situation and decide what would cause maximum damage and harassment to enemy shipping movements. We attacked ships berthed at quays but not further inland in case we inflicted casualties amongst Norweigan civilians. Our methods did not come from any text book but evolved from collected experience. On 6 May 1945 we were briefed and ready at our aircraft. A duty officer arrived. "OK, it's off, it's all over. Take these bombs off and put them away," he announced.'

APPENDIX 1

Civilians and the Home Front

WORLD WAR TWO affected every single person in the UK, from babies to the very old. Food shortages meant many people keeping chickens or growing their own vegetables. Vast numbers of citizens contributed willingly to the voluntary services. No one's life would be unchanged. Here are the memories of a few who lived in the West Highlands and islands at the time.

Donald Black was a schoolboy on Lismore in 1940, which was a quite backwater with only the occasional puffer or steamer visiting. 'One sunny morning in the late summer of 1940 all this changed: suddenly and quietly there appeared ships of all sizes and all nationalities. The rattle of anchors dropping brought us children to the 'cnocs' – the hill-tops – and we arrived at school hours late as we were witnessing momentous events. From that extraordinary morning the Firth was filled with shipping for five long years.

'After a convoy was attacked in December 1940, artillery sites were selected on the island. The public hall was commandeered by a squad of Royal Engineers who built Nissen huts for the Army personnel. A week or so later landing craft beached at Achuaran discharging more guns and trucks. A much larger and more heavily armed site was set up on 'Druim-ban' in the more northerly part of the island – a magnificent vantage point. Our quiet green little island had been turned into an armed camp. We were designated a 'Protected Area', which meant no-one could get on or off without identification. At the pier there was a check point and again at the North Pier in Oban.

'RAF and Naval personnel arrived and a camp was built

Oban ARP Volunteers with commandeered (Rolls Royce) Ambulance at Kilmore. (Black)

Home Guard pipe band marching along Oban Esplanade, 1944. (Palmar)

'Salute the Soldiers', an all-services parade held at Corran Green, 10 June 1944, which included the local BB, Guides, Sea Rangers and Scouts. (Hunter)

at Achnacroish next to the pier. Their job was to attach balloons to convoy ships. Some of the names of ships had an air of far away places, such as *City of Benares, San Demetrio, City of Exeter*. Some time in 1941 the American ships appeared for the first time. The crews came ashore to play baseball and soon "us-kids" were introduced to a great novelty – chewing gum.

'Just as suddenly and abruptly, as it began the bustle of these long-gone years was over – the Firth of Lorne was once again empty. How many of the crews had gone to their deaths? We shall never know. Only the shadows and memories, only the deserted camps and gun emplacements remained. The great ships were gone – they came no more.'

Dorothy Grimwood's husband was with 209 Squadron RAF, who came to Oban in 1939. 'When I arrived in Oban in October I had never been any further north than South Yorkshire, and this was the first time I lived away from East Anglia. We couldn't go far having no transport but enjoyed walks in the surrounding area. At first I wouldn't go shopping without my husband, as I found it very difficult to understand the accent, but I found everybody very kind. I soon made friends with other airmen's wives. We used to

For the inhabitants of the Hebridean islands, the war years meant disruption but also, oddly, a kind of prosperity. Many of the servicemen who were stationed on these islands were intrigued by the way of life they encountered, with traditional trades and tools still very much in evidence. Here, RAF Balivanich on Benbecula is seen under construction to the left of the photograph. (Griffiths)

go down to the quay and buy a whole cod for 2/6. It would feed my husband and I for three days.'

Nora Kirkpatrick was a young wife and mother at Oban in wartime. She recalls 'We had to queue for everything. People would join queues in the hope of getting things like fish and meat.' Nora once joined a queue and no one around was sure what was on offer. After a very lengthy wait she discovered people were queuing for vaccinations!

Marshall Draper was a Post Office telephone engineer which, along with many other jobs, was a reserved occupation. He set up communication links for Observer Corp posts around Oban, Kilmelford and Easdale, and helped establish links to the military on Lismore, Tobermory, Tiree, Barra and to Loch Na Keal on Mull. In case of invasion they had to store axes alongside telephone lines at certain locations.

Some of the men of the Mull Home Guard, photographed at Salen in the early 1940s. (Mull Museum)

Isabel Black was in the ARP at Oban. She recalls being at a dance in Oban when news came in of the Clydebank Blitz. She and other ARP girls had to rush in their long skirts to the ARP office, ready to leave for Clydebank, although in the end they did not get orders to go. One young London schoolboy evacuated to Oban joined the ARP. His name was Tony Benn, later a well known Member of Parliament and Cabinet Minister.

Donald McKinnon was a fourteen-year-old schoolboy on Tiree when the construction of the RAF camps began. 'It was strange to hear so much English being spoken and to meet Irish, Welsh and Englishmen. Any unoccupied houses were taken over by the RAF. Prosperity of a sort came to the island.'

Christine (Lamont) Reid, was at Tobermory High School during the war. 'I can remember days when we took

A class of schoolchildren on South Uist on Wings for Victory day, 1943, during a visit from some Canadian airmen. (Fitzgibbon)

Domestic Science classes out of doors. We would sit knitting things like socks for the forces. We would look down on all the activity in Tobermory Bay with warships coming and going. Through the Guides we would collect sphagnum moss for the Red Cross.'

Hugh MacLean, a crofter on Tiree, was a member of the Home Guard. He recalls, 'The RAF challenged the Home Guard to a shooting contest. The Tiree men won very convincingly. The Home Guard officer was also the Duke of Argyll's factor on the island. After the victory he announced, "I'm very proud of your shooting today. I know you are probably all poachers, but I'm still very proud today."'

Mark Faccenda had a Scottish mother and Italian father. As his parents moved back and forth between the countries some children were born in Italy, some in Scotland. When war came one brother was in the Royal Marines while another who was brought up in Italy's warmer climate served in the Italian Army. One night in 1941 an Oban police sergeant arrived to tell Faccenda he was being interned. He was a friend, and when he handed Faccenda over to the authorities at Dunoon he was in tears. Faccenda's mother was prevented from living in Oban, despite being Scottish, because of the military presence in the town. The Faccendas had been one of the first Oban families to have a radio pre-war but this was taken from them by the authorities. Eventually an Oban builder said he had a job for Mark and he was released from internment on the Isle of Man.

On Benbecula Mollie Pringle spent six months living with her father, Squadron Leader Walter, CO of the RAF on the island in 1944. She 'occasionally' went to school at Torlum but much preferred the education of fishing, illicit flights in aircraft, highland games and attending 'hectic' dances with locals. Her brother also enjoyed using cricket nets which were available in an empty hangar.

On the ferry to Oban Leonora Burden, a WAAF at Tiree, met a young woman who boarded at Mull and told her she had been a close friend of Adolf Hitler and that she had shot herself in the head the day war begun. (Mrs Burden didn't believe her, but this was Unity Mitford who died at Oban Hospital in 1947 from meningitis due to the bullet which had never been removed from her brain.)

APPENDIX 2

Hebridean Ferries

THERE could be no story of the West Highlands and Islands in wartime – or at most other times – that did not acknowledge the role of the famous ferry company, David MacBrayne Ltd (as it was at the time of the war). The ships of MacBraynes continued to be a lifeline to the Hebrides during World War Two, although they were also

The MacBraynes steamer King George V *before she departed to serve at Dunkirk.* (McNeil)

Making for Tiree. (Weatherall)

SS Hebrides, *which was more used to carrying cattle than people, at Coll.* (McKinnon)

Lochnevis *in wartime grey coming into Oban.* (West Highland Steamer Society)

called into service in locations far from their traditional ports of call. In January 1940 the old paddle steamer *Gondolier* was stripped of all her fittings and engines, towed to the Royal Navy base at Scapa Flow and sunk to form part of an underwater barrier. Both the *Lochgarry* and *King George V* were heavily involved in the evacuation from Dunkirk, on one return from which the *King George* was dive bombed by Luftwaffe aircraft and almost sunk. At the time she was carrying over 1000 troops and 100 tons of ammunition. After this she spent most of the war ferrying troops to large liners off Gourock. The *Lochgarry* became the only MacBraynes vessel lost in action when, during a terrible storm on 20 January 1942 she sank on rocks off the Rathlin Islands while on her way from Glasgow via Oban to Torshaven in the Faroe Islands on war service with the Ministry of Transport.

The former Oban cruise ship *Princess Louise* was badly damaged in a bombing raid on Greenock in May 1941. Another temporary casualty was the *Lochshiel*, which ran from Glasgow to Kinlochleven via west Mull. She was partially sunk at Mingarry Pier in March 1942.

Due to extra wartime demands the McCallum Orme and Co vessel *Hebrides* was lent to MacBraynes to assist with carrying passengers and supplies to Tiree, Lochboisdale and Castlebay. The *Clydesdale* also made this run but when she relieved on the Stornoway run there were vociferous complaints about the unsuitability of the vessel to carry beasts, let alone humans.

Of the other vessels used around the islands, the *Ulster Star* was from time to time chartered by MacBraynes as a cargo vessel. The last paddle steamer in the MacBraynes fleet, the *Pioneer*, was requisitioned by the Admiralty in June 1944 to become a headquarters ship at the RN base at Fairlie. The *Lochnevis* spent some time on naval duty in wartime grey as a mine layer. The *Lochaline* was used as a RN examination ship at Rothesay and the *Saint Columba* spent the war as an accommodation vessel on the Clyde for boom defence personnel.

With the war nearing an end in 1945, the valiant old *Hebrides* struck rocks in the Gunna Sound between Tiree and Coll on 31 May and had to be towed into Gott Bay.

Tribute to the Groundcrews

RAF groundcrew at work outdoors. Work continued in all conditions. (Solecki)

I T HAS BEEN ESTIMATED that there needed to be eight men or women working on the ground for every member of aircrew in World War Two. Insufficient testimony has been paid to these members of the RAF. The great successes that were achieved by the RAF could not have been possible without their long, long hours of devoted service. Here are just a few memories of people who served on Scotland's west coast and the Hebrides.

Tiree, like Benbecula and Stornoway, had specially shortened hangars to lessen the effect of gales. Joe Sylvester and George Cooper were with 8518 Servicing Echelon. Servicing work was carried out in oilskins, sou'westers, white polo neck sweaters, balaclavas, sea boot socks and gum boots. Field service caps were buttoned under the chin. The Servicing Echelon on Tiree often worked seven days a week. Ken Salt of 281 Squadron ground crew will never forget servicing aircraft engines with propellers going full blast in a cold gale only inches from his nose.

Bob Spinks was a cook in the RAF at Tiree in 1941 working at first from a croft and then at the airfield. The construction workers organised a boxing contest with the RAF. Despite training runs from Balemartin to Scarinish the RAF lost every fight to the construction men (from Glasgow and Ireland mostly). As an NCO driver with 206 on Benbecula, Tom Blue had the task of getting the island girls to RAF dances. He almost came to grief once trying to explain to Gaelic speaking crofters why he wanted their daughters to accompany him in his truck.

Tom Broomhead was a corporal Radar operator at Borve Castle in 1945 (Chain Home Low Station). They tracked

RAF groundcrew on Benbecula.
(Allison)

all aircraft including huge numbers of US planes returning home. Like all airmen they continually sought eggs from crofts. He once filled an oil drum with eggs to take home on leave to Sheffield. Joe Griffiths was a Navigator with 206 Squadron on Benbecula. 'I marvel at the wealth of experience that existed, especially in the maintainance and mechanical departments of 206. Some had been "boy entrants" and had learned their trade and crafts well. Our aircraft were well cared for and very seldom did anyone return to base with engine problems.'

Andy McNab was with 228 Flying Boat Squadron at Oban. 'We worked on the 'boats out on the water and were taken by launch from Kerrera to the 'boat we were to work on. We used to hang on by wrapping our legs round the small platform that came down from the leading edge of the main plane and work only with our hands. We soon became quite proficient – otherwise you would end up in the sea which would be tricky if you couldn't swim. All tools were supposed to be tied to you but most of us didn't bother.'

The silenced guns. A poignant image of the guns on the decks of captured U-boats as they were shepherded into ports such as Lochalsh, Oban, Tobermory and the Clyde in May and June 1945. (McDonald)

Conclusion

WHEN the War in Europe ended and the struggle in the Atlantic finally ceased, the world owed a great deal to the merchant seamen, the Royal Navy crews the and the RAF Coastal Command airmen who had perished in so many thousands. From Scotland over the sea to Canada and Russia, and onwards to all parts of the globe, they lie in unmarked graves, many fathoms deep. They may have no headstones but their deeds did buy time. Time for the Allies to build and re-group. Time for invasions to be planned. The sacrifice and squandered youth brought vital food and supplies – the very food of life and the sustenance for a war to liberate Europe – to British shores.

The U-boats did in fact make a last desperate attempt to break through into inland waters off the west coast of Scotland, and only devastatingly successful tactics applied by the Royal Navy and RAF Coastal Command prevented them causing havoc. No fewer than six U-boats were sunk in and around the Hebrides in the last year of the war: on 9 August 1944 U484 was sunk midway between Skerryvore and Barra Head by a Royal Navy frigate and corvette and a Sunderland of 423 Squadron RAF; two U-boats were sunk off Kintyre in January and February 1945; and in March 1945 HMS *Conn* was involved in two U-boat sinkings in Hebridean waters, the second twenty miles north-east off the Butt of Lewis on the same day U722 was sunk six miles north-west of Canna by the frigates *Byron*, *Fitzroy* and *Redmill*.

For all concerned World War Two was a momentous time. The majority of service men and women completed their service and left their war postings by 1946. However a deep legacy was left in the West Highlands and islands.

Improved roads were built to bring heavy loads for the war effort. RAF airstrips and vastly improved aircraft designs led to previously unimagined access to and from the mainland. Small islands benefited greatly too with the adaption of the landing craft design into mini ferries. The whole world too began to open up. Long range aircraft so vital to Coastal Command now ushered in the era of intercontinental travel.

Troopships returned to their bread-and-butter of emigration and immigration. For years so many young people left it seemed as though there might be another Highland clearance. Nothing, however, changed as much as attitudes. The Battle of the Atlantic literally affected the whole world. People left farms and cities all over Canada, the US, Australia, New Zealand and many other nations, and crowded into this small group of islands on the fringe of Europe. For the most part the locals welcomed this international, cosmopolitan invasion of their rural communities; business was given a boost, many lifelong friendships were formed, and as returning servicemen enthused about the Highlands and Hebrides, the demand for holidays would grow and pass on through the generations.

Scots served world-wide in every campaign of the war. As they returned home aspirations, tastes and social attitudes would never be those of 1939 again. Tales of opportunity and employment tempted many to venture far from the land of their birth. Perhaps the most profound changes were in the attitudes of and to women, with so many tasks being taken on in the military and civilian fields with vitality and success.

Acknowledgements

COUNTLESS PEOPLE have helped me in one way or another with this research. I would like to thank my family and the following and apologise to any I have omitted. Hugh Andrew and Donald Reid of Canongate. M Adam, J Aikman-Smith, F Ainslie, R Aitken, K Alllan, W Allan, W Allardyce, J Allison, M Allison, A Anderson, E Anderson, J Anderson, T Andrew, A Andrews, E Andrews, M Angel, R Anstey, F Armitage, F Ashberry, C Ashcroft, D Atkinson, K Atkinson, W Austin-Bishop, M Aves, J Ayers, J Ayling, T Bacon, W Badlan, E Baillie, K Bainbridge, G Bainbridge, F Baldwin, A Banks, R Banks, D Banton, M Barbarski, A Barker, A Bassett, A Bates, T Beesley, J Bell, T Benn, A Bennett, F Bentley, A Bergius, T Birch, A Bishop, R Bishop, R Blaber, D Black, I Black, N Black, G Blamey, B Blatchford, T Blue, T Boba, J Bond, A Bonnamy, T Bowell, W Bowen, T Boyd, K Brakes, A Bridger, M Breingan, T Block, M Brewer, M Brodie, H Bromley, D Brooks, V Brooks, H Brookes, R Bradford, A Bridgewater, T Broomhead, B Brinkley, P Brown, R Brown, W Brown, J Browrigg, J Brunton, D Bryan, H Bryce, W Bryden, S Bunney, L Burdon, R Burrage, G Butler, S Butler, A Burke, E Burke, P Buttery, G Calder, D Campbell, G Campbell, W Campbell, R Capon, R Card, R Carlisle, M Carmichael, C Carpenter, B Cave, E Chadwick, D Chaffe, A Chesworth, M Chilton, E Christie, L Clark, B Clarke, P Clarke, D Cobb, L Cobb, D Cockburn, P Collier, D Conacher, J Connell, E Cooper, D Courtney, R Cowey, J Creal, K Croft, V Crolla, H Crossley, J Crummey, P Currie, T Currie, L Curson, A Dagg, D Dagg, I Darling, R Davis, S Davis, J Davenport, T Dawson, N Dewdney, D Dews, W Dickie, W Diamond, F Dolman, A Donald, J Doern, A Dowmunt, G Downey, C Drabble, A Draper, M Draper, P Duncan, P Dunlop, R Dyer, C Eastbury, D Eastwood, C Edwards, P Eiles, S Ellerington, D Elms, L Emerson, T Emmington, K Emmott, J Entwhistle, M Eves, H Evans, J Evans, T Evans, G Evelion, M Faccenda, A Faulkner, R Fielding, C Fisher, F Fitzgibbon, H Forbes, J Ford, J Foord, J Fowler, I Fraser VC, L Frewer, R Frick, R Galer, A Garvie, J Garside, G Gates, N Geal, P Gethens, O Gill, G Gillfillan, W Gillan, H Gillies, S Goddard, P Godding, K Goodwin, L Gowans, J Glebocki, W Grant, D Gray, A Green, H Gregory, R Gribble, J Grifith, D Grimwood, J Grimwood, M Groombridge, D Grumbridge, I Grundy, F Hall, I Hall, R Hall, C Hallett, C Hamilton, F Hamp, D Hanson, H Hanson, K Harper, R Harrington, J Holliday, C Hart, A Hartley, J Harvey, T Harvey, F Harris, R Harris, E Harrison, H Harrison, J Hatfield, B Head, A Hendrie, F Heppell, P Hewlett, W Higgs, E Hill, T Hill, B Hillard, V Hodgkinson, J Hoey, T Holden, H Holderness, N Holdsworth, G Holleyman, J Holliday, D Holloway, F Holmes, J Holt, J Hodson, B Hood, J Hood, R Hood, O Hope, T Howard, G Howlett, G Hudson, P Huggins, H Hughes, T Hughes, D Humphreys, S Hunt, C Hunter, H Hunter, G Hynes, D Illingworth, F Insole, B Jameson, L Jamieson, L Jefferson, A Jenner, F Jenkins, D Jones, I Jones, M Jones, H Jurd, N Kayley, A Kemp, E Kilshaw, M King, N Kirkpatrick, J Kjolner, R Knight, N Knox, A Lacy, L Lambert, W Lamont, S Lane, G Lanzetter, J Lee, D Legg, T Lennox , B Lenton, M Lekawa, B Lewis, M Lewis, P Lidiard, J Liddy, B Lindsay, T Lloyd, E Lotocka, C Low, K Lunn, M Lutkin, G Maddis, D Mahoney, G Maier, A Mann, M

Martin, B Martyn, N Marshall, R Mason, J Mathews, M Mathieson, N Maynard, L Meidzibrodski, E Middleton, S Middleton, H Midgley, I Miller, R Milliken, J Milewski, A Mills, J Mills, M Mizen, M Moffat, A Monaghan, B Monk, C Monk, R Moorwood, T Morley, I Morrison, D Morrows, J Mowbray, J Montgomerie, Lord Monro, W Morrison, D Moxley, A Muir, G Murphy, M Murray, R Murray, J Mc Allister, D McAulay, J MacAuley, G McCaldon, H McCorquodale, R McCulloch, D McCusker, D McDonald, B MacDonald, R McDonald, S McDonald, A McDougall, Miss McDougall of McDougall, A MacEachan, B McEwan, D MacFarlane, D MacFie, R McGill, D McGillivray, M McGillivray, R McGillivray, M McGrail, R McIntyre, A McKenzie, N McKenzie, C McKinnon, D McKinnon, M McKinnon, D McKirdy, A McLaren, R McLachlan, D MacLean, J MacLean, H MacLean, M MacLean, D MacLeod, D McLundie, A McNab, C McPhee, L MacRae, G Nash, J Neil, S Neil, J Neilson, K Nichol, K Nicholson, W Nimmo, J Oliver, L Olsen, D Orr, S Ost, T Osborne, S Overend, B Owen, W Paddon, F Page, P Palmar, P Palmer, H Parker, S Parkin, J Parrish, C Paterson, G Peacock, C Pearce, G Pearman, S Pelling, R Pemberton, D Penlington, D Pepper, T Pettigrew, K Phillips, G Pickles, A Polakowski, D Polglaze, B Poloniecki, G Porazka, I Porter, H Pratt, N Preston, M Pringle, A Proctor, J Pryzbylski, G Purchase, P Rackcliff, R Radford, P Readie, C Reid, D Reid, D Ridley, J Roberts, R Roberts, J Robertson, G Robinson, H Rodgers, J Romanes, L Ross, P Routliffe, T Rowland, T Rowley, J Roy, J Russell, M Ryder, W Salt, D Sadler, H Sanford, G Saunders, H Saunders, J Scannell, A Shanks, G Shaw, P Shute, T Shuttleworth, S Simmonds, W Singleton, D Shepherd, J Shepherd, N Short, R Simpson, S Slight, P Sloman, A Smith, G Smith, H Smith, R Smith, W Smith, M Snell, D Snow, W Snape, J Solecki, C Southall, E Southwell, A Sparke, H Spencer, E Spinks, J Springthorpe, P Sprules, G Starreveld, A Steffen-Olsen, N Stephenson, I Stewart, J Stewart, A Stuart, W Stevenson, K Stoker, D Stone, F Styles, A Sutters, A Swain, J Sylvester, T Takarangi, S Taylor, J Templeton, C Terris, A Thomas, R Thomas, N Thomson, K Thompson, B Thornton, F Thorpe, J Tiller, I Timothy, D Titchiner, C Titcombse, E Tippet, R Toy, G Traub, P Travel, D Travis, G Trevers, M Tuckwell, C Turner, T Twelvetrees, P Tylee, M Valbonesi, P Vernon, B Vibert, G Vincent, B Vout, H Wakelin, K Walker, R Walker, A Wallace, A Ward, D Warren, G Watkins, R Watson, T Watson, B Weatherall, P Webb, L Webster, C Wedgewood, D Wells, P Wells, A Westgarth, G Whitamore, B White, J Whitley, P Whitworth, R Wickens, C Willington, D Williams, P Williams, S Williams, W Williams, T Winter, K Wintle, G Wilson, J Wilson, T Wilson, P Wilson, E Wood, F Wood, P Wood, H Woods, P Wooton, D Wright, E Zarudski, S Ziomek, RAFA Airmail Magazine, ASR/MCU Association, DEMS Gunners Assoc, Airmail Magazine, Navy News, RAF News, Scottish Memories, Oban Times, Oban Star, East Anglian Times, Aviation News, Air Historical Branch MoD, Coastal Forces Newsletter, Imperial War Museum, Argyll and Bute Council, Free French Assoc, 48 Sqn Assoc, Mitchel Library, Oban Library, Bellshill Library, Flypast, Catalina Assoc, LCT Assoc, Indian Ocean Flying Boat Assoc, Carmelite Monastry Oban, WW2 Radar Reunion, Coastal Command Halifax Assoc, 228 Sqn Assoc, Tropic Tusker Assoc, 206 Sqn Assoc, 220 Sqn Assoc, 271 Sqn Assoc, 422 Sqn Assoc, 423 Sqn Assoc, FAA Assoc, 36 Sqn Assoc, PBY Catalina Assoc, West Highland Steamer Society, RAAF, RNZAF, Canadian Defence Forces, Sikorski Museum, Warship World, Oban War and Peace Museum, Maritime Regiment, Polish Wings, WAAF Magazine, Yours Magazine, Evergreen magazine, Ships Today, Saga Magazine, Royal Commission on Historic Monuments Scotland, Royal Mail, Oban War and Peace Museum, Mull Museum, Museum of Islay Life, Portree Museum, Staff at Websters Photographers Oban and Waltons, Klick Bellshill.

Looking north-north-west from the top of Ceann A'Mhara on Tiree. (Gill)